Abstain from Every Form of Evil

Edited by Mike Willis

Truth
Publications

*Taking His hand,
helping each other home.*
™

ISBN 10: 1-58427-398-4

ISBN 13: 978-158427-398-1

This material was originally published in the May 17, May 31, June 7, and June 14, 1979 issues of *Truth Magazine* then published in different workbook formats after that time. Its present form has the following history:

First Printing: 2009

Second Printing: 2014

Truth Publications, Inc.
CEI Bookstore
220 S. Marion St., Athens, AL 35611
855-492-6657
sales@truthpublications.com
www.truthbooks.com

Table of Contents

The Authority of the Bible in Ethics

Guthrie D. Dean

Authority refers to "the power or right to act or command." Ethics has reference to "a set of moral principles or values; the principles of conduct governing an individual or a group." The chief priests and elders of the people came to Jesus and asked Him, "By what authority doest thou these things? and who gave thee this authority?" (Matt. 21:23). Though they themselves may not have been honest at heart, at least they recognized two things: (1) the need for religious authority; and (2) the fact that such authority must come from the proper source. Jesus, of course, taught by the authority granted to Him from the Father. The will of God, as revealed in the Bible, is our authority in doctrine and practice. It serves as the Christian's guide in dealing with human conduct. As Paul said to Timothy, ". . . that thou mayest know how thou oughtest to behave thyself in the house of God, which is the church of the living God, the pillar and ground of the truth" (1 Tim. 3:15).

The Bible Is Authoritative

In every situation we should learn to answer these Bible questions: "What is written?" Paul tells us, "All Scripture is given by the inspiration of God, and is profitable for doctrine, for reproof, for correction, for instruction in righteousness: that the man of God may be perfect, throughly furnished unto all good works" (2 Tim. 3:16-17). Peter writes, "According as his divine power hath given unto us all things that pertain unto life and godliness, through the knowledge of him that called us to glory and virtue" (2 Pet. 1:3).

We can realize how authoritative His word is from the fact that it will serve as the criterion by which we will be judged in the last day. Jesus stated, "The word that I have spoken, the same shall judge him in the last day" (John 12:48). The apostle Paul speaks of the judgment as "the day when God shall judge the secrets of men by Jesus Christ according to my gospel" (Rom. 2:16). (Paul's gospel, of course, was the gospel of Christ.) At the opening of the books in Revelation 20, the dead are` judged out of those things which are written in the books, according to their works (Rev. 20:12).

Though the standards of men may change and though the presumptuous may "call evil good, and good evil," and "put darkness for light, and light for darkness" (Isa. 5:20), the word of the Lord is settled forever, in heaven (Ps. 119:89). It is the rule by which we are to live; for it will definitely be the standard by which we are to be judged.

The Bible Offers a Pattern for Human Conduct

God's word offers clear principles to help the Christian make decisions in all areas of conduct. Gambling, for instance, is not dealt with per se, but there are principles which relate to the saint's action in such matters. Abortion may not be specifically dealt with, but the principles which require chaste behavior will take care of the problem before it arises. And the sacredness of life is upheld throughout the Scriptures. The New Testament is not designed to be a book of "thou shalts" and "thou shalt nots," but there are no circumstances that we face which are not covered therein. The Bible offers a clear voice and throws light on a straight path. It contains "present truth" for "such a time as this" (2 Pet. 1:12; Esth. 4:14). We are told that the grace of God that brings salvation has appeared unto all men, "teaching us that, denying ungodliness and

> Though the standards of men may change; and though the presumptuous may "call evil good, and good evil," and "put darkness for light, and light for darkness" (Isa. 5:20), the word of the Lord is settled forever, in heaven.

worldly lusts, we should live soberly, righteously, and godly, in this present world" (Titus 2:11-12). And note again what Peter wrote: "according as his divine power hath given unto us all things that pertain unto life and godliness, through the knowledge of him that hath called us to glory and virtue" (2 Pet. 1:3).

The world about us makes little effort to follow the principles of the word of God, and many even scoff at its authority. But the Christian has no other alternative but to submit to the Lord. If we reject His standard, we are in the same position that Simon Peter was when he asked: "Lord, to whom shall we go? thou hast the words of eternal life" (John 6:68). In matters pertaining to our morals, we must subscribe to the will of God. The apostles, under fire, remarked, "We ought to obey God rather than men" (Acts 5:29). We are not to be conformed to this world, but transformed by the renewing of our minds (Rom. 12:2). We are admonished, "If we then be risen with Christ, seek those things which are above, where Christ sitteth on the right hand of God. Set your affection on things above, not on things on the earth. For ye are dead, and your life is hid with Christ in God" (Col. 3:1-3). We should continue to look up and keep our eyes on Jesus. In this world of sin and lawlessness, the outlook may be dark, but the up-look is always bright.

The World Rebels at Divine Authority

The sinful world has always condoned such practices as dancing, immodest apparel, profanity, gambling, sexual immorality, and the use of alcohol. This is why godly parents have a continuing responsibility to train their children in the way of the Lord. This is why all of God's people are to watch and pray. That which is accepted by the world becomes a double threat to the saint. Young people, especially, do not want to be "different" from their peers. So the challenge to "come out and be separate" (2 Cor. 6:17) becomes even greater as more and more vices are made legal by man's laws and become "respectable" in the eyes of society.

Abortion, drug abuse, pornography, fornication, adultery, and homosexuality are being legalized by a godless generation. As more sins are sanctioned and made legal, the bigger the problem becomes for our country, for the average law-abiding citizen, and for all God-fearing people who are but strangers in a hostile world. But faithful Christians will continue to swim upstream, even though the rest of civilization may be rushing headlong into the sea of destruction.

Man may be smart enough to split the atom, invent all sorts of gadgets, fly backwards, and walk on the surface of the moon, but he has no authority to legalize sin and speak for God! Philosophers, sociologists, authors, scientists, psychologists, psychiatrists, denominational theologians, legislators, government officials, school teachers, college professors, special interest groups, Hollywood, Las Vegas, and Broadway entertainers, the television, and other mass media must not be allowed to become the Christian's standard and authority in ethics!

They cannot and they do not speak for me. Like Joshua of old, I say, "As for me and my house, we will serve Jehovah" (Josh 24:15, RV).

This Is No Time for Compromise

Whatever we do in word or deed we are to do all in the name and by the authority of Jesus Christ (Col. 3:17). Only His truth will make men free (John 8:32). And the truth is the word of the

Lord (John 17:17). (As we go forth with the truth we can afford to give no quarter to sin, yet we must continue to show patience and compassion toward the sinner. After all, our service and our worship must always be governed by two divine principles: spirit and truth [John 4:23-24].)

But this is no time for the trumpet to give an uncertain sound. This is no age for fence-straddling on matters affecting our morals and spiritual welfare. Today we certainly do not need soft preaching and compromise. And it is no time for silence on moral issues.

"I have set thee a watchman unto the house of Israel; therefore, thou shalt hear the word at my mouth, and warn them from me" (Ezek. 33:7). God made this statement to Ezekiel when Israel was being torn asunder by idolatry and immorality. It was during the period when the religious leaders had violated God's laws and were putting no difference between the holy and the profane, between the unclean and the clean (Ezek. 22:26). God's law in every age has been set up to distinguish between things that differ and approve of that which is excellent (Phil. 1:10). When the same prophet (Ezekiel) foretold the return of Israel from captivity, he recorded this admonition: "And they shall teach my people the difference between the holy and the profane and cause them to discern between the unclean and the clean" (Ezek. 44:23). God's word does that for us today, and we dare not compromise its truths. It is high time for all Christians to unsheath the sword of the Spirit and move forward with the fight against moral decay. You are to "cry aloud, spare not, lift up thy voice like a trumpet, and show my people their transgressions, and the house of Jacob their sins" (Isa. 58:1). Let us always remember that "the battle is the Lord's" (1 Sam. 17:47). And if God be for us, who can be against us (Rom. 8:31)?

Questions

Matching

_____ 1. Authority
_____ 2. Ethics
_____ 3. The church
_____ 4. The Scriptures
_____ 5. The grace of God
_____ 6. The world
_____ 7. My affection

A. Not to be conformed to this

B. The pillar and ground of the truth

C. On things above

D. The power or right to act or command

E. Profitable for doctrine, reproof, correction, and instruction

F. Principles of conduct governing an individual or a group

G. Teaches us to live soberly, righteously, and godly

NOTES

_____

_____

_____

_____

_____

_____

True or False

_____ 1. The Jewish leaders felt there was no need for one to act by proper authority.

_____ 2. We will be judged by the word of God.

_____ 3. The standards of morality set by men never change.

_____ 4. Something must be specifically condemned in the Bible before it is sinful.

_____ 5. Jesus alone has the words of eternal life.

_____ 6. During the days of Ezekiel some were making no distinction between the holy and the profane.

Discussion

1. Different people follow different standards of authority in the area of morality. Describe how the following standards of authority are used by some to justify their actions.

a. Peer pressure: _____

_____

_____

b. Philosophers, psychologists: _____

_____

_____

c. Entertainment field: _____

_____

_____

d. Government officials: _____

_____

_____

2. What should be our standard of morality? How do you reach this conclusion? _____

_____

_____

3. What are some ways we can be guilty of compromising God's standard of morality? _____

_____

_____

4. What can the following individuals do to uphold God's standard of morality?

   a. Preachers: _____

   b. Elders: _____

   c. Parents: _____

   d. Christians: _____

   e. Myself: _____

The Basis of Christian Ethics

Norman Midgette

While attending the University of Richmond, Virginia, I was required to take a course in Classical Greek. It was a study of Plato's *Euthyphro*, his *Apology,* and *Crito*. The setting was Greece; the story was about Socrates, and the time approximated that of Malachi. The writings were of Socrates' philosophy, teaching, trial, and death.

Socrates

Many who write on ethics consider Socrates the "father of moral philosophy." A brief analysis of the reasoning which led to his death and the reasoning of others who tried to convince him to escape death shows the weakness of trying to use human wisdom alone to decide what is morally right and wrong. To study ethics is to study what is morally right and wrong. It also is a study of the reasoning used to determine what is right or wrong. If there is a difference between ethics and morality it is very slight. Webster suggests that "ethical" may imply the involvement of more difficult and subtle questions of rightness, fairness, and equity.

Socrates

Now to the moral reasoning of Socrates as reported by Plato. Suppose you are a teacher trying to live a good life and do what is beneficial for your fellow countrymen. But some of them dislike you and consider you a danger to society, though there is no proof. You are arrested, tried, and condemned to death in a way that is unjust. While you are awaiting execution, your friends offer you an escape that will give you a longer life to continue with your family. So you consider the offer. You know that most people think you should escape and that you are guilty of no crime. You have not harmed anyone, but have only tried to help your country. If you live you can continue to teach and do good; furthermore, your family and friends need you. Should you take the opportunity and escape? Socrates said, "No! I cannot escape." He drank the hemlock and died. However, before he died he gave us some of the rules he followed in deciding what was morally right for him. Here are the main ones. (1) Moral decisions cannot be decided or affected by emotion but must be settled by reason. (2) We should never act in such a way as to harm anyone. By escaping, he reasoned, he would be harming the state. (3) Always keep a promise. He reasoned that by staying in Greece, when he was free to go elsewhere, he was "promising" to keep the laws of the country. (4) Always obey your superiors. He considered his country as his parents and teacher. He would not disobey its laws. (5) He said moral questions could not be answered by a public vote of the majority of people. The fact that most people thought he should be free did not justify his escaping.

But his friends reasoned he should escape, and here, in part, is their reasoning. (1) Socrates believed he had been "called" to teach by the god Apollo, and that should weigh more heavily than any other consideration. However, Socrates argued that *what is right* and what is *commanded by the gods* are not synonymous. They also reasoned: (2) Your teaching is for the good of the state. If you surrender and do not teach, you are not really helping the state but hurting it. Socrates recognized and acknowledged that conflict in his thinking, but further reasoned that there are times when one standard had to take precedence over another. Socrates' self-imposed standard of morality in this given set of circumstances led to his death. His friends' ethical reasoning by their self-imposed standard would have led to his escape. Conflicting judgments, conclusions, and actions have always followed where moral standards of right and wrong have been left to the human will. It is the same today.

Today

One group today contends that the ultimate criterion for determining what is morally right is the standard of *good*. This is called by the moral philosophers the teleological theory. To them an act is right if and only if the standard and the act will produce or is intended to produce more good than evil or bad. An act is *wrong* "if and only if it does not do so." But, these moralists differ on the question, "Good for whom?" John Stuart Mill argues it has to be the greatest *personal* good. The reasoning of Hitler made mass murder of the Jews morally right because he reasoned it was for the greatest national good. Such reasoning is logically possible under this theory of morality.

A second theory says that the first theory is fallible. It argues an act may be morally right if it does not promote the personal or general good as judged by men. To them, an act toward others or self is morally right if it (a) *keeps a promise*, (b) is *just as commanded by God* or *by the state*. However, they also have a problem of trying to decide if (1) "I must always do what is just," or if (2) "in *this particular situation* I must do what is just." Those who follow this theory of morality are called *deontologists*. There is no absolute answer for them, so they also become a law each to himself.

A third group today says simply, "If it is the loving thing to do, it is right." This moral theory has made greater inroads into the seminaries, church

leadership, and moral religious writings than either of the first two. Armed with this moral standard, a preacher for the United Church in Chatham, Ontario, made available to young unmarried couples a room for sexual revelry. This was shortly after the book *Situation Ethics* became popular. This philosophy of morality says love, not God, determines what is right and wrong.

God

There is another alternative to this moral dilemma. It is a standard much easier to understand. It is the standard that will establish the greatest good for all: not just for now, but for eternity. There is a single standard of ethics for the Christian, for all Christians. But, equally important are the reasons this single standard must be accepted.

One reason is the *limitation and ignorance of man*. This should be evident to the smart men who are floundering around in the various moral theories with all their unanswered questions and conflicts. There is no agreement among them and no possibility of agreement unless, that is, everybody agrees to submit his thinking to the thinking of one man. Experience shows that this is not going to happen.

God pointed out in the Bible what many should have learned from the repeated experiences: We are limited in our ability and wisdom. God has said, "It is not in man that walketh to direct his steps" (Jer. 10:23), yet the "way of a fool is right in his own eyes" (Prov. 12:15). We are further informed, "Every way of a man is right in his own eyes" (Prov. 21:2). But the fact remains that we know not what is right and best without help from God. When men alone have tried to give that help and moral direction, confusion has resulted. So one of the major reasons we need a standard is that we are unable within ourselves to know the answers. And it is not a matter of willful ignorance, but rather a matter of moral inability.

The second reason we need that standard established by God is *His inherent authority*. The irreligious and those with their backs toward God will not accept this fact. It will not be accepted until one is willing to take a good look at the evidence for God and His rights and give it a fair hearing. Once His being and works are accepted,

> **Our only standard of moral authority for the exercise of moral rightness is found in the doctrine of Christ. It is His word that will finally judge (John 12:48).**

His authority to direct and guide of necessity follows. The last verse of Hosea says, "Who is wise, and he shall understand these things? prudent and he shall know them: for the ways of the Lord are right, and the just shall walk in them: but the transgressors shall fall therein" (Hos. 14:9). Because of His authority and supreme position over the universe, *His ways are right*.

In the coming of Christ "all authority" (Matt. 28:18) was given to Him by God, and that is why our only standard of moral authority for the exercise of moral rightness is found in the doctrine of Christ. It is His word that will finally judge (John 12:48).

That foundation on which Christian ethics are built is the revelation of God, the Bible. And the reason we gladly accept this basis is our mortal inability to know and the right of God. Peter gave our marching orders and pointed our direction when he said, "We must obey God, rather than men" (Acts 5:29).

Socrates had his rules, John Stuart Mill his standard, and Hobbes and Hitler rationalized morality to their satisfaction. But Christ has revealed God's will, and not only is it more beneficial and humanly considerate than all the rest, but, most of all, He has the authority to enforce it and hold us accountable for it.

NOTES

Questions

Definitions

1. Ethics: _____

_____

_____

2. Socrates: _____

_____

_____

3. Teleological theory: _____

_____

4. Deontologists: _____

_____

5. Situation ethics: _____

_____

6. Inherent authority: _____

_____

7. Christian ethics: _____

_____

Where's the Verse?

1. "It is not in man that walketh to direct his steps." _____

2. "The way of a fool is right in his own eyes." _____

3. "Every way of a man is right in his own eyes . . ." _____

4. "Who is wise, and he shall understand these things? prudent and he shall know them: for the ways of the Lord are right." _____

5. "All power has been given to me." _____

6. "We must obey God rather than men." _____

Situation Ethics

Weldon E. Warnock

Ethics means "a series of rules and laws and principles by which we act and which tell us what to do." But "situation ethics" is not geared to rules and regulations. This system of ethics refuses to be circumscribed by rules and laws. It says there is nothing right or wrong. Moral behavior is relative, not absolute. Decisions depend on the situation at hand, rather than law. It is also called the "new morality," "contextualism," "ethical individualism," "casuistry," as well as some others. But regardless of what one calls it, it does not make the system any more respectable.

Joseph Fletcher's Views

Joseph Fletcher, a professor of social ethics, an Episcopalian, and a well-known proponent of "situation ethics" stated: "As we shall see, *Christian* situation ethics has only one norm or principle or law (call it what you will) that is binding and unexceptionable, always good and right regardless of the circumstances. That is 'love'—the *agape* of the summary commandments to love God and the neighbor" (*Situation Ethics,* 30).

Fletcher further wrote, "For the situationist there are no rules—none at all" (55); "Circumstances alter rules and principles" (29); "all laws and rules and principles and ideals and norms, are only *contingent*, only valid *if they happen* to serve love in any situation. . . . the Christian chooses what he believes to be the demands of love in the present situation" (30, 55). "The new morality, situation ethics, declares that anything and everything is right or wrong, according to the situation" (124).

There are three approaches to follow in making moral decisions according to Fletcher (18-26):

1. Legalistic. He says, "With this approach one enters into every decision making situation encumbered with a whole apparatus of prefabricated rules and regulations."

2. Antinomianism. "Over against legalism, as a sort of polar opposite, we can put antinomianism. This is the approach with which one enters into the decision making situation armed with no principles or maxims whatsoever, to say nothing of rules."

3. Situationism. "A third approach, in between legalism and antinomianism unprincipledness, is situation ethics. . . . The situationist enters into every decision making situation fully armed with the ethical maxims of his community and its heritage, and he treats them with respect of illuminators of his problems. Just the same he is prepared in any situation to compromise them or set them aside in the situation if love seems better served by doing so. . . . The situationist follows a moral law or violates it according to love's need."

Fletcher allows stealing, lying, adultery, and anything else that the law of God prohibits. His thinking is shown in the following statement: "But situation ethics has good reason to hold it as a duty in some situations to break them, any or all of them. We would be better advised and better off to drop the legalist's love of law, and accept only the law of love" (74).

On pages 164-165 of Fletcher's book, Fletcher captures the attention of the readers about a German woman separated from her husband at the Battle of the Bulge and imprisoned in the Ukraine. While in prison she learned that her husband, who was a prisoner of war, had been released from another camp and had located their two children in Berlin.

There were two reasons the Russians would release a prisoner: (1) severe medical treatment or (2) pregnancy. She persuaded a Russian soldier to impregnate her in order to be released. Following her pregnancy she was released and joyfully united with her family. All loved her and the child born out of adultery. Fletcher lauds this as a loving act, the law against adultery being superseded by the situation at hand.

From what Fletcher said, we can readily see where situationism is coming from. It is a philosophy of liberalism, pragmatism, relativism, and individualism that arrays itself against the word of God and makes a mockery out of the Bible.

Jesus and Situation Ethics

In his book, *The Christian New Morality*, O. Sydney Bar stated, "The new morality is biblical morality. Behind it lies the authority of Jesus Christ Himself" (6). Situationists use for proof (?) Jesus's defense of His disciples regarding the charge brought against them by the Pharisees of eating grain on the Sabbath (Matt. 12:1-8). The Pharisees considered the plucking of the grain and the rubbing it in their hands to separate the grain from the chaff, work, thereby violating the Sabbath.

Jesus vindicated His disciples, according to situationists, by His approval of David's breaking the law of God in eating the forbidden shewbread

Joseph Fletcher

(1 Sam. 21:6; Lev. 24:9). They tell us that human welfare has preference over the laws of God. By sanctioning David's action, Jesus in turn justified His disciples and established a precedent for all time to come, they reason.

But Jesus never approved or encouraged the violation of God's law under any circumstances. Eating on the Sabbath was not a violation of God's law. Sin is a transgression of law (1 John 3:4). Jesus never sinned (Heb. 4:15). Hence, He never violated a law of God. Neither did He encourage His followers to sin or try to justify their sins.

Jesus said, "Whosoever therefore shall break one of these least commandments, and shall teach men so, he shall be called the least in the kingdom of heaven: but whosoever shall do and teach them, the same shall be called great in the kingdom of heaven"(Matt. 5:19). From this passage we can see clearly what Jesus thinks of lawbreakers. Adherence to God's laws is emphasized over and over in the Bible.

J.W. McGarvey, commenting on Matthew 12:3-5, stated:

Jesus expressly admits that what David did was unlawful; and some have supposed that he here intends to justify it on the ground of necessity, and then to argue that his disciples, though guilty of violating the law of the Sabbath, are justifiable on the same ground. There is no doubt that on this ground David excused himself for eating the shewbread, and they the Pharisees did the same for him. But it cannot be that he who refused to turn stones into bread when tortured by a forty days' fast . . . would approve such a violation of law as David was guilty of. Neither can it be that he allowed his own disciples while under the law to break the Sabbath. If Christians may violate the law when its observance would involve hardship or suffering, then there is an end of suffering for the name of Christ, and an end even of self-denial.

But it is clear that by the Pharisees David's act was thought excusable, otherwise they could have retorted on Jesus thus: Out of your own mouth we condemn you. You class your act with David's; but David sinned, and so do you. Now the real argument of Jesus is this: David, when hungry, ate the shewbread, which it was confessedly unlawful for him to eat, yet you justify him: my disciples pluck grain and eat it on the Sabbath, an act which the law does not forbid, and yet you condemn them (*The New Testament Commentary*, 103-104).

In regard to the priest's profaning the Sabbath by their religious services in the temple (v. 5), McGarvey says,

Having silenced his opponents by the argument *ad hominem*, he next proves by the law itself that some work may be done on the Sabbath day. The priests in the temple were required to offer sacrifice, trim the golden lamps, and burn incense on the Sabbath; and these acts required manual labor. In this case, the general law against labor on the Sabbath was modified by the specific law concerning the temple service. The term "profane" is used, not because it was real profanation, but because, being labor, it had the appearance of profanation. The example proves that the prohibition of labor on the Sabbath was not universal, and as it was not, it might not include what the disciples had just done (*Ibid.,* 104).

Opposition to Fletcher's Ethics

Peter Wagner, writing in *Eternity Magazine*, February 1967, said:

1. He (Fletcher) says that love is the only norm of ethics. But what is love? How is its context determined? . . . We need the rest of the Bible to guide us as to just what the law of love expects from us.

2. Love, for Fletcher, is neighbor love. But this is only the second table of the law. The first is love of God. . . . It is impossible for us to love our neighbor properly without first loving God, and we in turn show our love to God by obeying his commandments.

3. . . . be impossible for him to define with any preciseness a 'situation' . . . To be able to predict all involved in a moral decision in every case, especially in a crisis of life, is too much to expect even of an ethics professor to say nothing of the man in the street.

4. . . . (Fletcher) bases his law of love on revelation. But he does not tell us what criterion he has used to select this particular fragment of revelation and reject the rest. There must be some norm which tells him he ought to believe revelation when it speaks about love, but he need not believe it when it speaks about lying, fornication, or stealing.

Wagner, as you can see, gets right to the heart of the problem and forcefully destroys the very foundation on which Fletcher builds his theory.

James M. Gustafson, professor of Christian ethics at Yale University, wrote in *Christian Century*, May 12, 1966, the following: "He (Fletcher) states that the situation is determinative. However, he is never very careful to designate what constitutes a 'situation' . . . If one says that the situation plus love makes for the right action without being clear about what love is and is not, one has a simple formula, a radical ethic in both substance and method."

Henlee H. Barnette, professor of Christian ethics at Southern Baptist Theological Seminary, wrote, as quoted in *The Situation Ethics Debate* (136): "Love alone, or situation ethics, is characterized by a one-sided methodology

NOTES

_____
_____
_____
_____
_____
_____

in arriving at moral decisions. It is a misplaced emphasis, a false polarization in Christian ethics."

John Macquarrie wrote in his book, *Three Issues in Ethics* (33-35), the following:

> One of the most telling objections against situationism is that it is a fundamentally and incurably individualistic type of ethic. Paul Ramsey is correct in his warning that "no social morality ever was founded or ever will be founded, upon a situational ethic."

> . . . As well as suffering from individualism, radical situational ethics suffers from the allied vice of subjectivism. The situationist seems to be compelled by the theories to assume an extraordinary degree of moral sensitivity and perceptiveness in those who are expected to read the demands of the situation.

> . . . The situationist is less than realistic in the extent to which he is willing to recognize the weakness of human nature and the fact that even our conscience can be distorted.

William Barclay stated, "If we insist that in every situation every man must make his own decision, then first of all we must make man morally and lovingly fit to take that decision; otherwise we need the compulsion of law to make him do it" (*Ethics in a Permissive Society*, 81).

Ladies and gentlemen, there is no way that a Bible believer can embrace situation ethics and remain true to the Bible. The Bible and situation ethics are on different planes and operate on different channels. Situation ethics or the new morality sets aside the Bible whenever man wants to and injects his own judgment in its place.

Consequences of Situation Ethics

There are several adverse consequences of the situation ethics philosophy.

1. Destroys respect for the Bible. The Bible claims itself to be an all-sufficient guide (2 Tim. 3:16-17; 2 Pet. 1:3). It saves us (Jas. 1:18), and by it we will be judged (John 12:48). The situationists tell us we need not be concerned about what the Bible teaches, but just let love have its way.

2. Makes love and law exclusive. For the situationist it is either love or law. For the

Christian, it is both law and love. Jesus said, "If ye love me, ye will keep my commandments" (John 14:15, ASV).

3. Deifies man. It makes man his own God. Man decides what to do and when to do it. He becomes his own standard. Jeremiah tells us that it is not in man to direct his own steps (10:23). God knows what is good for man, and therefore, we shall follow Him (Deut. 6:24).

4. Obscures right and wrong. The system implies that each one is to do his own thing as he interprets the problem or issue in a particular situation. There is nothing inherently right or wrong, they say, but it must be judged in context on the spur of the moment.

5. Presumes each act will turn out well. What if the woman in the concentration camp who got herself impregnated in order to be released had been resented by her husband and children? Things like this are always the possible consequences of the arbitrary and subjective acts in situation ethics.

6. It encourages permissiveness. At least Fletcher's approach encourages permissiveness. Listen to him: "Does any girl who has 'relations' . . . outside marriage automatically become a prostitute? Is it always, regardless of what she accomplishes for herself or others—is it always wrong? Is extramarital sex inherently evil, or can it be a good thing in some situations?" (Ibid., 17-18) To Fletcher, extramarital sex may at times have intrinsic value. A man decides for himself if this is true.

Conclusion

Actually, situation ethics is not something new. Catholics have had for centuries their form of situation ethics, called "mental reservation," enabling them to lie whenever they deem it necessary. Protestants have always practiced situation ethics in setting aside God's command of baptism for the man on his death bed or the man in the desert.

But faithful Christians have always obeyed God in all things (Acts 5:29). Christians wait for the way to escape (1 Cor. 10:13), pray often for strength and guidance (Jas. 5:16; Phil. 1:9-10), and study the Bible regularly to know God's way

(Ps. 119:11). With rapturous acclaim, they say with the psalmist, "O how love I thy law! it is my meditation all the day" (Ps. 119:97).

Questions

Yes or No?

_____ 1. Is situation ethics also called the "new morality"and "ethical individualism"?

_____ 2. Was Joseph Fletcher, the author of the book *Situation Ethics*, an atheist?

_____ 3. Should love be the motivating factor behind our obedience to God?

_____ 4. Does situation ethics have only two rules?

_____ 5. In the realm of morality, can one be either a legalist, an antinomian, or a situationalist?

_____ 6. Is the first law to love our neighbor?

_____ 7. Can one be true to the Bible and embrace situation ethics?

_____ 8. Does situation ethics presume that the decision based on love will always turn out well?

_____ 9. Have Catholics and Protestants ever been guilty of practicing situation ethics?

What Would You Advise?

1. A young couple has been dating regularly for a number of years. They love each other very much. The young man has been called to go to war. On the night before his departure, he pleads with his girlfriend to have intercourse with him, for he may not return. He reasons that if she truly loves him she will. What advice would you give this young girl? _____

_____

_____

_____

2. The members of a family have been told that their mother is dying of cancer. The family members know how upsetting such news would be to their mother. Someone suggests that they tell her everything is fine, so as not to cause her added grief. What advice would you give this family?

_____

NOTES

_____

_____

_____

_____

_____

_____

_____

What is Wrong with the Following Statements?

1. In 1 Samuel 21, David and his men violated God's law when they ate the shewbread. But Jesus approved of their action because of their need for food. When there is a higher law we can set aside a lower law. _____

    _____

    _____

2. Rahab the harlot lied to protect the two spies in Jericho. But, according to James 2, she was justified by God in this act. Therefore it is acceptable if we lie to protect someone from great harm. _____

    _____

    _____

3. Matthew 23:23 teaches that we should not be concerned with the ceremonial laws of the Bible, but what really matter are the higher moral laws like love and mercy. _____

    _____

    _____

Drug Abuse—Works of the Flesh

James R. McCain, M.D.

Dolly and Harry gave a schoolboy some white stuff that looked like stardust. He ran with great speed to the yard, where he lay in the grass and, looking up into the blue heavens, dreamed of taking trips where he could have juice, fags, and a businessman's high. Doesn't make much sense, does it? These sentences were constructed using slang names for drugs that are being used today! Methadone, heroin, codeine, morphine, cocaine, amphetamines, marijuana, barbiturates, LSD, alcohol, tobacco and DMT.

Drug abuse is not just a problem for the underprivileged families and for the ghettos, but it is a problem for all society—the Christian family included. Drug abuse to the Christian should immediately bring to mind the "works of the flesh" in Galatians 5:19. "Now the works of the flesh are manifest, which are these: fornication, uncleanness, lasciviousness, idolatry, sorcery, enmities, strife, jealousies, wraths, factions, divisions, parties, envyings, drunkenness, revellings, and such like." Any and all of these works could conceivably be a resultant factor in drug abuse. But a Christian need practice only one "work of the flesh" to miss inheriting the kingdom of God. Among all the "works" mentioned in the above Scripture, "sorcery" stands out as the one that would embrace drug abuse. "Sorcery" is the translation of the Greek word for pharmacy. It primarily signifies the use of medicine, drugs, or spells. Other "works" such as uncleanness, lasciviousness, drunkenness and revellings very often are associated with drug abuse.

If we wanted to use one phrase to describe why people abuse the use of drugs, it would probably have to be because of its "mind-altering" effect. Here again Christians are taught to be sober—sober-minded. The word "sober" as used in 1 Thessalonians 5:6-8 (not drunken), 1 Peter 1:13 (gird up mind by being sober), and 1 Peter 5:8 (be sober, be watchful; your adversary the devil, as a roaring lion, walketh about, seeking whom he may devour) is translated from the Greek word *nepho*. This word *nepho* signifies in the New Testament "to be free from the influence of intoxicants." We must therefore be keen of mind, lucid, ever watchful, whereas the drug abuser is easy prey for the devil and will be devoured by the "roaring lion."

This lesson is being written in the hope that those who read it may be better informed about the dangers of the drugs that are being used today by our young people and even by older people. These drugs, which alter the mind and have the potential for causing organic damage, should be relegated to the devil and not be a part of the sober Christian's armor.

> The most prevalent drug used today is alcohol.

The most prevalent drug used today is alcohol. By definition alcohol falls in the category of being a food because it does contain calories. However, it has no nutritional value. It also can be categorized as a drug because it affects the central nervous system. Unfortunately, the term alcoholic does not apply to only the older generation. The average age for becoming an alcoholic is becoming increasingly younger and younger. There are even cases recorded of seven-year-old children becoming alcoholics. The average age a young person begins to drink alcoholic beverages is 13-14 years. The addictive years for alcohol are between ages 18 and 24 years. It takes a teenager fifteen months to become addicted; it takes an adult fifteen years to become addicted.

Twenty percent of the alcohol consumed by an individual goes into the bloodstream immediately; the remaining 80 percent goes in only slightly more slowly but once in the blood stream begins its tranquilizing effect, although at first it may seem to be stimulating. The amount of alcohol taken in, size of the individual, whether consumed with food, and how rapidly it is taken in determine how quickly the brain becomes depressed. If steady, heavy drinking persists, the brain can become anesthetized to such a degree that coma and death may result. The more chronic long-term effect of alcohol is seen to contribute to cirrhosis of the liver, gastric ulcers, heart disease, serious nervous and mental disorders, and even permanent brain damage.

Many homes are destroyed because of alcohol; many accidents are the direct result of alcohol consumption. There are several million so-called alcoholics in the world today, and a recent survey revealed that 68 percent of American adults drink at least occasionally. Twenty percent of those who drink become alcoholics. Forty-one billion dollars a year is spent on alcohol. Many young people are turning from other drugs to alcohol. The lowering of the legal age to 18 years has not helped the situation.

Some states are considering going back to age 21 as the legal age to buy intoxicating beverages. (Why not age 100?)

Marijuana is, at the present time, the second most popular and widely used drug. Marijuana is derived from the flowering tops and leaves of the Indian hemp plant, cannabis sativa. It has been known by man for nearly 5,000 years, but was not introduced into the USA as an intoxicating drug until 1920. Eight percent of the marijuana used in the USA comes from Mexico, with the rest coming from Africa, India, the Middle East, and the USA. It has been estimated that $100 million a year is spent on marijuana use.

It can be smoked, or a concentrate of it called hashish oil can be dropped on a regular cigarette or in food. It enters the blood stream and acts on the brain and nervous system. It works by affecting the mood and thinking process. Among other things it affects decision making processes. It makes a person highly vulnerable to other people's suggestions, often resulting in highly irresponsible activity. Marijuana use does not result in a physiological dependence (i.e., the body has to have it to function), but it does result in psychological dependence, therefore it is habit forming. Although medical science does not know all the effects of marijuana, since it is classified as a mind-altering chemical, society in general, and Christians in particular, should refrain from its use.

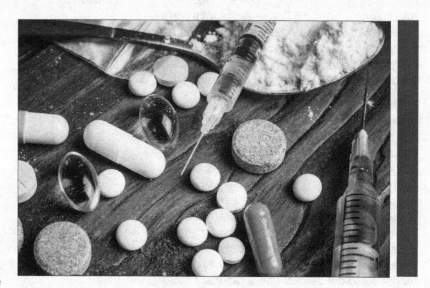

There is a group of drugs known as hallucinogens. The most popular one of these has been LSD (D-Lysergic acid diethylamide), developed in 1938 from a fungus, ergot, that grows as a rust on rye and other cereals. It is so powerful that a single ounce provides 300,000 average doses.

Another hallucinogenic drug is derived from the peyote cactus and is called mescaline. The Indians of northern Mexico have used it for years as a part of their traditional religious rites. Psilocybin, DMT, and STP are other hallucinogenic drugs.

The hallucinogens produce sensory illusions, making it difficult to distinguish between fact and fantasy. In large doses they may produce unreal sights and sounds, and users may describe "hearing" colors and "seeing" sounds. Senses of direction, distance, and time become disoriented.

Restlessness and sleeplessness are common symptoms. Tolerance to the drugs develops after prolonged use; therefore, larger and larger doses are required for the user to get the desired effect. And the effect is unpredictable and may result in "good" trips or "bad" trips.

Chronic use does not apparently cause physiological dependence but can alter the user's values and impair his power of concentration and ability to think. It is not known how LSD works, but it is thought to affect the levels of certain chemicals in the brain and to produce changes in the brain's electrical activity.

There have been reported many cases of panic and fear of losing one's mind: paranoia (feeling someone is trying to cause harm or control one's thinking); a recurrence of "the trip" days, weeks, or even months after having used the drug with the resultant fear of losing one's mind; and accidental death because the user thinks he can fly or float in the air, therefore leaps from great heights, etc. Although research has not proved it, the use of LSD becomes a high risk to pregnant women because of the possibility of chromosomal changes in an unborn child, causing defects.

Many volatile substances produce an intoxicated state when inhaled. Young children and adolescents are more prone to try these methods of distorting consciousness. These fall into three groups: (1) Commercial solvents such as roluene, benzene, acetone, carbon tetrachloride, and other volatile substances found in airplane glue, plastic cements, paint thinner, gasoline, cleaning fluid, nail polish remover, and cigarette lighter fluid. (2) Propellants in aerosols. (3) Anesthetics—chloroform, ether, etc.

The psychic effects of these may produce a high dreamlike state, drunkenness, sleepiness, disorientation, hallucinations, delusions, and stupor. Most sniffers do not recall the events that occurred while "under the effect." The young people who engage in this practice often have a history of delinquent activity. Because of the intoxicating effect that impairs judgment and motor function, many accidents occur, often fatal. Habitual use, depending upon the material, may cause lead poisoning (gasoline), kidney and liver disease (carbon tetrachloride), and tissue damage to the brain.

Another group of drugs on the drug abuse list are the depressants. These are chloral hydrate, barbiturates, clutethimide (Doriden), methaqualone (Quaalude), meprobamate (Miltown, Equanil), benzodiazepines (Valium, Librium). These drugs are widely prescribed by physicians for the treatment of insomnia, relief of anxiety, irritability, and tension. In excessive amounts they produce symptoms similar to that of alcohol. These drugs can cause physiological dependence. Taken with alcohol they can become lethal. Depressants are often used, particularly by women, as a means of suicide.

Stimulants are chemical drugs that excite the central nervous system. The most common are nicotine (tobacco) and caffeine (coffee and tea). Used in moderation they relieve fatigue and increase alertness. The stronger stimulants are cocaine, the amphetamines, and the anorectic drugs (appetite suppressants). All the stimulants produce mood elevation and a heightened sense of well-being. Chronic users feel stronger, more confident, decisive, and self-possessed. If given directly in the vein, they may produce a sudden sensation known as a "flash" or "rush." The protracted user, after getting a stimulating effect, may later lapse into a state of depression known as "crashing." As a result, another injection is given, and the condition may progress

NOTES

_____
_____
_____
_____
_____
_____

to delirium, psychosis, or physical exhaustion. Those in professions that require alertness for long hours often take stimulants (uppers) to stay awake. In some, a pattern of "uppers" in the morning and "downers" (alcohol or depressants) at night develops. It is not certain whether these drugs cause physical dependence, but very definitely they cause psychological dependence. There have been some fatalities among athletes who have undergone extreme exertion after taking moderate amounts of stimulants.

Cocaine is extracted from the South American coca plant and is currently used infrequently in the medical profession. When sniffed, snorted or given in the vein, it causes extreme euphoria. Because of its intense pleasurable effect, a strong psychological dependency may develop. The amphetamines are used medically for unusual states of sleepiness, appetite control, and hyperactive behavioral disorders in children.

The anorectic drugs such as Tennate, Presate, and Ionamin are used for appetite control and are less potent than the amphetamines.

When we say narcotic drugs, we think of heroin, morphine, paregoric and cocaine. Certain synthetic drugs such as Demeral and Dolophine are also considered narcotic drugs—painkillers. These definitely cause physical as well as psychological dependence. These drugs are being used by young people in the ghetto, as well as some middle-aged and older people who take them regularly to relieve pain. Heroin at first reduces tension and eases fears and anxiety. Following the exhilaration period, the user may sink into a stupor. Heroin decreases appetite, thirst, and the sex drive. Many habitual users, therefore, suffer from malnutrition. Heroin addiction is particularly lethal because it is such an expensive habit. A user may need to spend from $75-$100 a day to satisfy his needs. Therefore, oftentimes he has to resort to stealing and other crimes. Women often resort to prostitution. Those addicted to heroin and other narcotic drugs are by far the most difficult to cure because of withdrawal sickness. Once the drug has been withdrawn, the difficult task lies in keeping the user from picking up the habit again.

Abusive drugs are everywhere—in the grammar schools, high schools, the entertainment and professional worlds, and on the street. As responsible citizens and concerned Christians, we should be aware of the dangers of these drugs. They are truly, intimately, and unequivocally related to the "works of the flesh."

NOTES

_____
_____
_____
_____
_____
_____

Questions

Multiple Choice:

_____ 1. The word (a. uncleanness, b. sorcery, c. revellings) is from a Greek word signifying the use of medicine, drugs, spells.

_____ 2. The Greek word (a. *nepho*, b. *luo*, c. *bapto*) means to be free from the influence of intoxicants.

_____ 3. The most prevalent drug used today is (a. alcohol, b. LSD, c. Marijuana).

_____ 4. It takes a teenager (a. seven years, b. thirty-six months, c. fifteen months) to become addicted to alcohol.

_____ 5. The second most popular and widely used drug is (a. cocaine, b. marijuana, c. LSD).

_____ 6. Marijuana acts on the (a. circulatory system, b. respiratory system, c. nervous system).

_____ 7. Hallucinogens make it difficult to distinguish between (a. fact and fantasy, b. good and evil, c. light and dark).

_____ 8. Many volatile substances produce an intoxicated state when (a. smoked, b. injected, c. inhaled).

_____ 9. Chemical drugs which produce mood elevation and a heightened sense of well-being are known as (a. depressants, b. barbiturates, c. stimulants).

Make a List.

1. List some of the slang names for illegal drugs being used today._____

_____

2. List passages which you might use to show the sinfulness of drug abuse. _____

_____

3. List some of the diseases that come from the extended use of alcohol._____

_____

4. List some of the effects of hallucinogens. _____

_____

5. List some of the effects of the use of volatile substances, such as sniffing airplane glue, nail polish remover, etc. _____

_____

_____

6. List some of the effects of heroin. _____

_____

_____

Agree or Disagree:

1. "Drug abuse is not really a problem for Christians." Do you agree or disagree with this statement?
    Why?_____
    _____
    _____
    _____

2. "Since marijuana has not been shown to be physically harmful, then there is nothing wrong with using it." Do you agree or disagree with this statement? Why? _____
    _____
    _____

3. "There is no danger of becoming addicted to drugs if they are prescribed by a doctor." Do you agree or disagree with this statement? Why?_____
    _____
    _____

4. "As Christians we should try to warn others of the dangers of drug abuse." Do you agree or disagree with this statement? Why? _____
    _____
    _____

Marijuana: A Righteous and Moral Activity?

Keith Clayton

In traveling around the country and meeting with people, I find a marked increase in the reported use of marijuana. Indeed, perusing the various periodicals and journals would seem to verify this very observation. In the August 7, 1978, issue of *U.S. News and World Report* magazine, we find the following statistics offered by Dr. R. Dupont, Jr.:

- 43,000,000 Americans have tried marijuana.

- 16,000,000 Americans are current users.

- Nine percent of high school seniors are daily users (because it is available to adults, it is available to adolescents—kec).

- Eleven of twenty college people have tried it.

- Two of twenty college people use it daily.

- Fifteen percent of all auto accidents are attributed to it.

I know personally people who seem to feel that marijuana use is not so harmful as some other people feel. Rather, it is really quite harmless and morally right. Their reasoning goes, "After all, I use it and I am not such a bad person!" "After all, I am OK!" But I pose this question: Since when has God ever determined righteousness and morality upon the basis of human actions and rationalizations? The answer is never; moreover, the Scriptures specifically state that it is not in a man who walks to direct his steps (Jer. 10:23). God has provided the only guide to "life and godliness" (2 Pet. 1:3) in the instrument of the Bible. "All Scripture is inspired by God and profitable for teaching, for reproof, for correction, for training in righteousness; that the man of God may be adequate, equipped for every good work" (2 Tim. 3:16-17). It is the Creator and not the creature that determines right and wrong, just and unjust, moral and immoral, and heaven or hell as a final abode of the spirit of man. Let us consider some Bible facts and principles that are pertinent to the subject.

The relationship of the righteous and Christ has to be one of respect for the name of Christ: an attitude of not wanting to do anything that would bring shame to the great and glorious

name of the Son of God, the King of kings. A good way to remember this is to understand the spiritual relationship between the Christian and Jesus. "Set your mind on the things above, not on the things that are on earth. For you have died and your life is hidden with Christ in God. When Christ, who is our life, is revealed, then you also will be revealed with him in glory" (Col. 3:2-4).

> The Christian and Christ are to be inseparable, and the Christian should not set his mind upon anything that Jesus would have no part of.

The Christian and Christ are to be inseparable, and the Christian should not set his mind upon anything that Jesus would have no part of. This is further elaborated on in Matthew 5:16 where application is made to the effect that people of the world should find in Christians a light to lead them to truth and Jesus: "Let your light shine before men in such a way that they may see your good works and glorify your Father which is in Heaven." Therefore, in order for marijuana smoking to be acceptable in God's eyes, it must do these two things: help keep Christians faithful and lead people to Christ. It does neither!

Marijuana use, according to Dr. R. DuPont, Jr., is a terribly deceptive practice. He further states (U.S. News and World Report, August 7, 1978), "Only the tip of the iceberg has been seen regarding the ill effects in health, social activities, family living and work performance. . . . The first illegal drug that young people adopt is marijuana. Then there is a hierarchy leading to heroin . . . the thing is that when people stop using drugs, they usually go back down these steps in reverse sequence. . . . We already know enough to say marijuana poses a substantial risk. Anyone who takes the drug and thinks nothing has happened to his body has lost his mind." As we can see, an expert, a member of the President's Drug Abuse Commission, explains that the possible effects of marijuana are near- ly all negative in nature. Certainly, we cannot see Jesus engaging in these things, nor can we

see Jesus through the person who practices the consumption of marijuana.

Marijuana stands condemned (without considering the evil companions who travel with it) because of the significant health hazards it presents. Marijuana, according to a special report in Time Magazine (January 29, 1979, 26), produces these adverse medical and health effects:

Immunity—Some studies have shown a marked reduction in white blood cell response, the body's prime defense against infection, in marijuana smokers.

Chromosomes—Human cell cultures from pot users have shown breaks in chromosomes carrying genetic information, or reduced numbers of chromosomes.

Many doctors believe, however, that some people can easily become psychologically dependent on the two drugs (marijuana and co- caine, kec) and the effects they produce.

Also, we find more negative evidence from the April 1978 issue of the Science Digest. I.R. Rosengard, M.D., researched the aftereffects of a total of 37,000 occasions of marijuana use by many individuals. The physiological effects found are as follows:

1. Increase in heart rate

2. Reddening of the eyes

3. Extremely hard on bronchial system . . . like rubbing sand paper on lung tissue.

4. Mental and motor performance impaired, many cases severely.

One conclusion reached by this doctor was this: "Marijuana is highly dangerous if used before or during the use of an automobile (to others who do not use it also, kec). If it were legal and use of it became widespread, accident rates would triple. It should never be legalized." Moreover, in a CBS documentary titled, "Reading, Writing, and Reefer," research showed that one marijuana "joint" is equivalent, in terms of respiratory system damage, to twenty- one tobacco cigarettes. Additionally, there was a great deal of concern for the development of the adolescent who participated in the use of marijuana (aside from the terrible health ef- fects). We can clearly see that marijuana is absolutely not productive rather, it is absolutely a destructive element to add to an already morally decaying society.

Obviously, the Bible does not mention marijuana by name; however, there are God-given principles which we can use to determine the acceptability of the use of this drug. Those principles are in addition to the ones previously mentioned regarding Christ/God's words that have a very direct bearing on the subject at hand. Marijuana is damaging to the body physically, mentally, and spiritually—this can be readily established. Then we consider God's will for our bodies and we discover: "What? Know ye not that your body is the temple of the Holy Ghost which is in you, which ye have of God, and ye are not your own?" There is no way a Christian, a lover of God, can use marijuana as a pleasure (reality modifier) and not endanger the attainment of a home in heaven, because he deliberately damages his body. The Bible gives us a strong statement of damnation and destruction against the sinner who condones such behavior. "Do not be deceived, God is not mocked; for whatever a man sows, this he will also reap. For the one who sows to his flesh shall from the flesh reap corruption, but the one who sows to the Spirit shall from the Spirit reap eternal life" (Gal. 6:7-8). If man gives in to unhealthy, sinful, sensual, and fleshly desires (unscripturally), then he or she cannot be controlled by God's word. Such a one cannot inherit the kingdom of God, according to the word of God (Gal. 5:19-21).

Let us listen to the words of Jesus in closing. Think of all the ill moral, mental, and bodily, effects of the use of marijuana (the fruits brought by its use), as we read the Savior's words in Matthew 7:16-19. "Grapes are not gathered from thorn bushes, nor figs from thistles, are they? Even so, every good tree bears good fruit; but the rotten tree bears bad fruit. A good tree cannot produce bad fruit, nor can a rotten tree produce good fruit. Every tree that does not bear good fruit is cut down and thrown into the fire." What kind of "fruit" is the consumption of marijuana? Can the child of God, the Christian, do anything except totally abstain and please his Creator? "But examine everything carefully; hold fast to that which is good; abstain from every form of evil" (1 Thess. 5:21-22).

NOTES

Questions

Who Said It?

1. "16,000 Americans are current users." _____

2. It is "not in man who walks to direct his steps." _____

3. "Set your mind on the things above, not on the things that are on earth." _____

4. "The first illegal drug that young people adopt is marijuana. Then there is a hierarchy leading to heroin."

   _____

5. Some of the effects of marijuana on the body are "increase in heart rate, reddening of the eyes, extremely hard on bronchial system . . . mental and motor performance impaired." _____

6. "Your body is the temple of the Holy Ghost." _____

7. "A good tree cannot produce bad fruit, nor can a rotten tree produce good fruit." _____

Fill in the Blanks.

1. It is the _____ and not the _____ that determines right and wrong.

2. "Let your _____ shine before men in such a way that they may see your _____ _____ and _____ your _____ which is in Heaven."

3. Some studies have shown a marked reduction in _____ _____ cell response in marijuana smokers.

4. Human cell cultures from pot users have shown breaks in _____ carrying _____ information.

5. Smoking marijuana is like rubbing _____ _____ on lung tissue.

6. One marijuana "joint" is equivalent, in terms of respiratory system damage, to _____ tobacco cigarettes.

7. Marijuana is damaging to the body _____ , _____ , and _____ .

8. One who gives in to unhealthy, sinful, and fleshly desires cannot inherit the _____ of _____ .

True or False.

_____ 1. Ten percent of all automobile accidents are attributed to marijuana.

_____ 2. God, not human actions and rationalizations, determines righteousness and morality.

_____ 3. A Christian should not want to do anything that would shame the name of Jesus.

_____ 4. One can take marijuana and not do serious harm to his body.

_____ 5. There would be no basic danger to society if marijuana were legalized.

_____ 6. We can experiment with marijuana and not be endangered by it.

_____ 7. Marijuana is wrong because of the evil fruits it produces.

_____ 8. The Christian should totally abstain from marijuana.

The Problem of Drink

Jack Kirby

Christians agree that drunkenness is sinful. Paul lists it as one of the works of the flesh (Gal. 5:21). Here it is clearly indicated that the impenitent drunkard "shall not inherit the kingdom of God." The same apostle also declares that a local congregation is not to extend to or maintain its fellowship with a drunkard. "But now I have written unto you not to keep company, if any man that is called a railer, or a drunkard, or an extortioner: with such an one no not to eat" (1 Cor. 5:11). Therefore, if, in facing the problem of the drinking of alcoholic beverages, the extent of it were drunkenness, then the solution would be plainly set before us. There is more to the matter, however, than just drunkenness.

In the United States today, over 65 million persons above the age of twenty use alcoholic beverages. Seven million of these are "problem drinkers" and 3 million are addicted to alcohol. One million are chronic alcoholics. Drinking is a problem which faces every one of us —even those who are "teetotalers." Another aspect of the problem arises when we realize that the annual cost of America's liquor bill is nearly $10 billion. That is more money than all the people and institutions in our country spend in a year's pursuit of educational and benevolent purposes.

Perhaps someone reading this has wrestled or is wrestling with this problem in a very personal way. The habit of drink has fastened itself upon you, and you struggle to control the situation. Let it be understood now that the purpose in these remarks is not to cry, "Shame on you." We face a problem here that involves all of us directly or indirectly; therefore, I have no choice but to deal with that problem carefully and directly.

In some ways, it is hard to receive a fair hearing on the matter of drink. This is true because of the extreme thinking that prevails about the problem. Some feel that to discuss drinking is infringing upon personal liberties. Thus, because of these prejudices and the obvious fact that the liquor industry is "big business," it becomes difficult to lead a group of people into such a frame of mind that the problem can be approached in a realistic fashion.

Drinking Is a Very Real Problem

Is it possible that any of us lives so far removed from the world about us that we see no real danger? Do we feel that some excitable preachers are crying, "Wolf!" when there is no wolf?

> Perhaps someone reading this has wrestled or is wrestling with this problem in a very personal way. The habit of drink has fastened itself upon you, and you struggle to control the situation.

We cannot blink our eyes at the well-documented fact that drinking and, as a result, drunkenness are on the increase in this nation. The Yale School of Alcohol Studies leaves no doubt on this point. Alcoholics are increasing at the rate of 50,000 a year. Problem drinkers (those who need a "bracer" two or three times during the course of a day) are growing at the rate of 200,000 a year. Not even the most fanatical supporter of a man's right to drink can ignore the simple fact that, out of the 1 million people killed in highway accidents, one-quarter of these died where liquor was directly involved. This figure does not include the number who were injured or maimed, nor can we translate the heartache and the heartbreak into numerals. Those involved in between one-fourth and three-fourths of the divorces obtained in this country have listed drinking as either the primary cause or a contributing factor.

When we view television, we receive the distorted impression that drinking is always pleasant, beneficial, and good. When we open many of our major magazines, we immediately become acquainted with "men of distinction" wearing roses in their lapels. The impression is left that success and efficiency in business, the professions, and in personal relationships go hand in hand with drinking. You are bound to succeed, provided you drink the right thing at the right time! This is another false impression.

The nature of the problem is impressed upon us by a survey conducted among college students. Two facts stand out: (1) Of those who drink, four out of five men and two out of three women began to do so before they entered college. This indicates that drinking originates in high school age groups. (2) The incidence of drinking among these students increased with each year that they spent in college. Thus, the habit of drinking is one that begins with young people. Any way you look at it, drinking (not just drunkenness) is a problem. In fact, it appears to be several different kinds of problems rolled into one. This is another reason it is hard to get a fair hearing on the subject of alcoholic beverages today. Will anyone deny that drinking is not a health problem? Can we say that the problem has no economic aspects? Is it not also a matter that concerns our law enforcement agencies? Yet, many will deny that drinking is a moral, religious problem! That simply means that some are saying: "It is my business if, when, where, and how much I drink." Exactly at this point issue must be taken.

Alcohol is a narcotic that removes inhibitions. By releasing these inhibitions, drinking makes for social ease and pleasure. Alcohol impairs reason, will, self-control, judgment, physical skill, and endurance. Drink is used primarily for psychological effect as a means of escaping unpleasant reality. Are we to believe that a beverage which does these things is not a maker of problems in human life? Shall we accept the idea that a thing which produces these results in our lives is not the concern of a Christian and of the church? Let us consider briefly these ideas and see a few of the religious implications that are involved in them.

The Releasing of Inhibitions

Just what does this mean? An inhibition is an eternally imposed curb on action; that curb is usually conscience, or it may be fear or dread produced by past experience. Some inhibitions bring shyness, cowardice, or other "unsocial" reactions. True, these need to be removed, or at least to be managed if not removed. Other inhibitions are called "social control" and grow out of our environment, training, and ideals. Thus, they constitute our standard of judgment and values. But drinking removes or lowers all inhibitions, both good and bad! The same power that can conquer shyness can also numb the conscience and encourage the breaking down of morality. It is entirely vain to argue that this is not a matter of concern to the church and to every Christian. If this is not a religious problem, then nothing is!

Drinking impairs reason, will, self-control, judgment, physical skill, and endurance. What remains of someone when these qualities have been removed? The extent of the removal of these qualities depends upon the amount of liquor which is consumed. But even "light" or moderate drinking can cause a person to be unfit for exacting physical and mental work. It is well-known that much of the absenteeism in industry is due to the consumption of alcohol. It has been demonstrated by actual tests that drinking a cocktail or two makes it necessary for the driver to have six more feet to stop a car than he would need before drinking or without drinking. Men may say, "It is my business when I drink," but if the child whose life is saved by that six feet is yours or mine, it becomes our business!

Alcohol is used as a means of escape from unpleasant realities. But such an escape from reality is temporary and can be achieved again only by another drink or by more drinking. Christian principles, when believed and followed in our lives, will enable us to face the realities of living and solve them permanently by the doing of God's will. Dodging the facts of life is not a solution to them, nor does dodging remove the realities that are with us.

The Case for Total Abstinence

Some questions have been discussed for centuries. There is often a revival of interest in them. They need to be studied anew and often.

Such is the question denoted by the heading of this section. This question should be studied in a manner as free from prejudice as possible. One should give due emphasis to "intellectual honesty." He should not be swayed by popular opinion. What does the Bible teach?

Did First Century Christians Have the Right to Drink Moderately?

Those who take a dim view of "total abstinence" have one thing in common: they all try to construct a case from the New Testament showing that moderate drinking of alcoholic beverages was permitted in the first century. Almost without exception they use 1 Timothy 5:23; Titus 2:3; and John 2:1-12. These, and some other passages, use the word "wine" in such a way as to indicate that Christians, on occasion, did drink it. They assume this was intoxicating wine. On this basis they try to construct a case for the Christian's moderate drinking of alcoholic beverages with divine approval. They fail in their assumption that all wine was of alcoholic content. Was it?

The word "wine" (Greek *oinos*) was a general word used to translate more specific Hebrew words. Sometimes it did mean wine of the intoxicating variety, but not always. Isaiah 65:8: "Wine is found in the cluster." There the word refers to the juice of grapes while they are still

on the vine! Josephus (*Antiquities*, Bk. 2, ch. 5, Sec. 2) tells of three clusters of grapes hanging from a vine, "and that he squeezed them into a cup which the king held in his hand; and when he had strained the wine, he gave it to the king to drink." These are but two of numerous recorded historical uses of the word "wine" when it could not possibly refer to an intoxicant.

Furthermore, the wine with alcoholic content was not strong except in cases of "mixed wine." Yeast, found in the hulls of the grapes, causes the fermentation of grape juice. When the alcohol content gets to approximately fourteen percent, the alcohol kills the yeast and the process of fermentation stops. Many times the process is stopped early so that the alcohol content is far less than the maximum fourteen percent. Canon Farrar says, "The simple wines of antiquity were incomparably less deadly than the stupefying and ardent beverages of our western nations.

NOTES
_____
_____
_____
_____
_____
_____

The wines of antiquity were more like syrups; many of them were not intoxicant; many more intoxicant in a small degree; and all of them as a rule, taken only when largely diluted with water. They contained, even diluted, but four or five percent of alcohol."

Some writers assume that there was no way of preserving the juice of the grape without fermentation in the first century. However, various ancient writers give different methods for so doing. The new *Zondervan Pictorial Bible Dictionary* says, "Means for preserving grape juice were well known: Cato, *De Agri Cultura*, CXX has this recipe: 'If you wish to have must (grape juice) all year, put grape juice in an amphora and seal the cork with pitch; sink it in a fishpond. After 30 days take it out. It will be grape juice for a whole year."

Thus, it is an unwarranted assumption to declare that all wines in New Testament days were alcoholic.

The Problem of Social Drinking

In our society today, social drinking constitutes a very real problem. Functions are attended where alcohol is served; business relationships often involve drinking; thus, many people have come to feel that drinking is a complement to good business and to social contacts. It is here that the importance of example and of Christian influence must necessarily enter the picture. Like it or not, accept it or not, face it or not, we are responsible for the influence we exert on others. Paul faced this question of influence in Romans 14. The individual may say, "I can drink and control my drinking." This may be very true. How about someone else who is weak, young in faith, or young in years and who may conclude from your example that drinking is good, and, while you can control yourself, he cannot and goes into drunkenness? Will the influence of social drinking actually lead men to obey Christ? Sincerely, do you feel that this type of influence and example are good for the young people? What will be—what is—the influence of the social drinker in the church of our Lord? Are those who continually engage in social drinking viewed by the world and by the church as among the most devoted, consecrated members of the body of Christ? Will they, should they, be chosen to serve as elders, deacons, or teachers for the instruction of the young people? These are questions that each one must answer from the depths of his heart before God. And the question of the influence of social drinking upon the children in a family cannot be lightly considered. A parent may never develop into an excessive or dangerous drinker, but how about the children? They may grow up thinking that to drink is the way of culture, the way of refinement, and a part of a normal, happy life; but will those children in their lives be just moderate drinkers? Young people are more vulnerable to the temptations of drink by the very nature of their immature development than the average adult. What example shall we set before them about the use of beverage alcohol? The Christian must face the responsibility that is here, as well as in other areas of life, and warn against the dangers of drinking.

Let us realize that no heavy drinker or drunkard—no alcoholic—ever deliberately started drinking to become that. Are not those today enslaved by alcohol the very people who began with the intention of reaping only the "benefits" of this narcotic? Are not they the very people who began with the intention of reaping only what liquor used in moderation could do for

NOTES

them—forgetting at the same time what drinking would also do *to* them? You may be a potential alcoholic, though you have never taken that first drink. You may be a moderate drinker today who could become an alcoholic tomorrow. You cannot know where the use of alcoholic beverage may ultimately lead you; therefore the danger is a stark, terrible reality. Yet every one of us—and the young people can here heed especially—must face the possibility of what drink can do as he asks the question: "Shall I drink?"

It has been our intention to point out that drunkenness is sinful. There are dangers connected with drinking. The influence of social drinking is not good. Drinking alcohol is dangerous to the body and society, as well as being sinful. We pray that each of us, when confronted by the problem of drinking, will determine by the help of God to chart that course which will not bring reproach upon the body of Christ, ourselves, and our families.

Questions

Definitions

1. Wine (Greek *oinos*, as used in 1 Tim. 5:23): _____

   _____

   _____

2. Excess of wine (Greek *oinophlugia*, as used in 1 Pet. 4:3): _____

   _____

3. Revellings (Greek *komos*, as used in 1 Pet. 4:3): _____

   _____

4. Banquetings (Greek *potos*, as used in 1 Pet. 4:3): _____

   _____

   _____

Multiple Choice

_____ 1. Over (a. 14 million, b. 35 million, c. 65 million) persons above the age of twenty in the U.S. use alcoholic beverages.

_____ 2. There are (a. 1 million, b. 3 million, c. 7 million) people in the U.S. who are addicted to alcohol.

_____ 3. Alcoholics in this nation are increasing at the rate of (a. 500, b. 5,000, c. 50,000) a year.

_____ 4. The habit of drinking is one that begins with (a. young people, b. middle-aged people, c. senior citizens).

_____ 5. Alcohol is a narcotic that removes (a. stains, b. infections, c. inhibitions).

_____ 6. Drinking a cocktail requires a driver to have (a. four, b. five, c. six) more feet to stop a car than he would have needed before drinking or without drinking.

_____ 7. Ancient people had (a. no way, b. different ways, c. only one way) of preserving the juice of the grape without fermentation.

_____ 8. As a Christian, I should be concerned about my influence on (a. all men, b. weak Christians, c. strong Christians).

_____ 9. The potential for becoming an alcoholic comes with (a. the first drink, b. the fifth drink, c. the tenth drink).

What's Wrong with These Statements?

1. "Television and magazine ads give an accurate and honest impression of drinking." _____

    _____

    _____

2. "Alcohol doesn't harm me." "I can control my liquor." "I don't get drunk." _____

    _____

    _____

3. "It's no one's business but mine if I drink." _____

    _____

    _____

4. "Jesus turned water into wine so it must be okay to drink it." _____

    _____

    _____

5. "Deacons are not to be given to much wine, so they can be given to a little bit." _____

    _____

    _____

6. "Paul told Timothy it was okay to use a little wine. So it is okay to drink a little just as long as I don't get drunk." _____

    _____

    _____

Smoking

Curtis J. Torno, M.D.

The recent release of the Surgeon General's second report on smoking reemphasized the health hazards of smoking. Those of us in the medical profession have recognized these hazards for a long time. Despite a few denials from those who desire to use tobacco and willfully refuse to face facts, the truth has long been evident to even a casual observer. A trained observer knows the hazards of smoking all too well.

Smoking one package or more (twenty cigarettes) a day will shorten one's life on the average by twelve years. A select committee of the American Heart Association chaired by Dr. William B. Kannel, the director of the Framingham Study, said, "325,000 premature deaths from heart disease can be directly attributed to cigarette smoking."

A study from the United States Public Health Service (USPHS) reported in 1977 that the lung cancer rate among female smokers was 101.4 women per 100,000 female population and 392.8 men per 100,000 among male smokers. Among nonsmoking females, the rate was 9.4 per 100,000 and 12.5 per 100,000 among males. This is very significant! The USPHS estimate is that nearly 75,000 of the 84,000 who die of lung cancer every year would not have died if they did not smoke. The cancer rate among female smokers is twelve times greater than it is among non-smokers, and among male smokers it is thirty-five times higher than male nonsmokers. That means that among smokers the lung cancer rate is 1 in 25 and among nonsmokers it is nearly 1 in 10,000. Significant, isn't it?

The Framingham Study of over 5,000 subjects for sixteen years has demonstrated conclusively that cigarette smoking is extremely hazardous to health. The overall death rate from all causes for smokers is twice that of nonsmokers in the same areas, in the same jobs, and from the same backgrounds. The USPHS calls smoking "the foremost cause of preventable disease and death in this country." The British Royal College of Physicians compares the effect of cigarette smoking to the "lethal power of great epidemic diseases such as typhoid, cholera and tuberculosis."

Among adult men, the smoking rate is down 25 percent, but among women the rate is up by about an equal amount. The greatest increase is among pre-adult girls and boys. Most of the increase in consumption has been among women and the very young. This is tragic, especially when as much as fifteen percent of those twelve years old and under smoke. The smoking rate is the highest of any age group among those between fifteen and twenty-one, both girls and boys. It is a paradox that the older, wiser, and best informed segment of our population is decreasing smoking while the uninformed and least wise are the ones that are consuming the most and taking up the habit at an increasingly young age.

The Christian should understand that not only can his smoking affect his health and cause early death, but it affects his children and those with whom he associates. Children whose parents do not smoke have only a fifteen percent smoking rate, but, among children whose parents do smoke, 85 percent also smoke. So not only do smoking Christians endanger their own bodies and souls, but affect and influence others, also.

The only bright side to this ugly picture is that it is possible to stop smoking! More than

> **Smoking one package or more (20 cigarettes) a day will shorten one's life on the average by twelve years.**

The study of British doctors is frequently quoted to illustrate a beneficial effect of stopping smoking on total mortality. Male doctors aged 35 to 64 years showed a fall in mortality of 12.4 percent in the years 1962-65 compared with 1953-57, whereas in the total male population, the fall was only 2.9 percent. Half of the doctors who smoked had given up smoking during these years, while those in the general population were said to have altered their smoking.

that, stopping causes a marked diminution in the health hazard and death risk. According to the American Cancer Society's study of more than 1 million subjects—the largest of the prospective investigations—male smokers had up to twice the overall mortality of nonsmokers, the risk being greater according to the number of cigarettes smoked and the duration of the smoking habit. Women smokers also had a higher mortality rate, but less than men. Those who had given up smoking before joining the study had *death rates that decreased according to the length of time since they had last smoked cigarettes*.

Those who used to smoke one to nineteen cigarettes a day showed a steady decline in risk, so that after ten years, they had the same mortality rate as those who had never smoked. Heavier smokers (more than twenty cigarettes a day) began to reduce their risk five years after stopping, but even after ten years their mortality rate was higher than those who had never smoked. In the ACS and other studies, mortality rates in the first year after stopping tend to be higher than those of smokers, because it is often illness that makes a person quit.

A recent report from the Framingham study provides support in that "men who gave up smoking after entry to the study had half the attack rate for coronary heart disease, excluding angina, compared with those who continued to smoke."

All of this should be encouraging to those who may have smoked and desire to stop. Basically, if one stops now, in ten years he has largely overcome the hazardous effect on his body. Of course, if one continues to smoke, he continues to run the increased risk of premature death.

Over 55 percent of all physicians have quit smoking, and now fewer than 20 percent of all physicians smoke at all. In a recent survey of over 10,000 physicians, 98 percent answered "yes" to the question, "Do you consider cigarette smoking as hazardous to health?" and two percent answered that they weren't sure yet. None answered the questionnaire that it was their opinion that there was no hazard to health in

NOTES

smoking. As the American Cancer Society poster says, "Maybe they know something you don't know." You could know and should know what a health hazard smoking is.

Anyone who thinks cigarette smoking is not harmful and hazardous to one's health cannot read the label on the package and cannot read the volumes of published material that are available. How many rational normal people would continue to eat cranberry sauce or tuna fish or candy if the package label said, "**Warning**: *consuming this material can be dangerous to your health"*? Yet, millions go on inhaling cigarette smoke despite the warning. What would happen to the sale of tuna fish if it could be proved that one in twenty-five of all people who ate tuna fish would develop lung cancer, while there were other people who lived in the same area and worked at the same jobs, but who did not eat tuna fish, and boasted a lung cancer rate of only one in 10,000? How many would continue to eat tuna fish?

This is the advice of a physician and almost unanimously the advice of any physician—stop smoking while you still can. Smoking cigarettes is a lethal habit that shortens your life, harms your influence, puts you in disregard to common sense and sound advice, and puts you in direct opposition to many New Testament principles. If you do not stop for your conscience's sake—please stop for your body's sake and the sake of those of our younger generation, who will be encouraged to smoke or not smoke by your example.

Questions

Fill in the Blank

1. Smoking one package or more a day will shorten one's life on the average by _____ years.

2. The cancer rate among female smokers is _____ times higher than it is among female nonsmokers.

3. The cancer rate among male smokers is _____ times higher than it is among male nonsmokers.

4. The greatest increase in smoking is among _____ girls and boys.

5. _____ percent of those twelve years and under smoke.

6. The smoking rate is the highest of any age group among those between _____ and _____.

7. Children whose parents do not smoke only have a _____ percent smoking rate, but, among children whose parents do smoke, _____ percent also smoke.

8. If one stops smoking now, in_ _____ years he has largely overcome the hazardous effect on his body.

9. Smoking cigarettes is a lethal habit that _____ your life, _____ your influence, puts you in _____ to common sense and sound advice, and puts you in direct _____ to many New Testament principles.

Why Do You Agree or Disagree with These Statements?

1. "Smoking is a slow way to commit suicide." _____

_____

_____

2. "Jesus said in Mark 7:15 that there is nothing that can enter man and defile him, but rather what comes out of man is what will defile him. Since smoking enters the man, it does not defile him."

_____

_____

3. "Smoking will harm one's body, and one should not harm his body since it is the temple of the Holy Spirit." _____

_____

_____

4. "That smoking harms the body is just the opinion of men and the opinions of men should not be bound upon us." _____

_____

_____

5. "Smoking harms our influence with people who might not be Christians." _____

_____

What Would You Do?

1. You are out with a group of teenagers and one of them pulls out a cigarette and lights it up. He then begins to pass the pack around and everyone else begins to imitate his example. What would you do when the pack reaches you? _____

_____

_____

2. In a meeting with a group of people, someone asks, "Do you mind if I smoke?" What would you say? _____

_____

_____

_____

Lesson 8

Fornication and Adultery

Thomas G. O'Neal

An older preacher friend told me several years ago that fornication was the most often committed sin. I am inclined to agree. An article I read in the *Nashville Banner* (September 9, 1973, 11) said the Playboy Foundation commissioned The Research Guild Inc. to make a survey, the results of which were published in *Playboy* in October of 1973. Those surveyed were 2,026 in number over 17 years of age; 982 were men, and 1,044 were women. Seventy-five percent of the single women surveyed said they had had sexual relations before they were 25; 32 percent of the married men under twenty-five said they had had sexual relations with partners besides their wives since they had married, and 24 percent of married women said the same thing. Current statistics if available would not show an improvement.

Added to the practice of sin, now there are some preachers who are giving their voice to the sanction of fornication and adultery. While they would deny that they favor adultery or fornication, their voices and pens say otherwise. Concerning the exception of Matthew 19:9, Leroy Garrett said Matthew "inserted that exception on his own, and that Jesus never said it" (*Restoration Review*, November 1978, quoted by Mike Willis in *Truth Magazine*, Vol. 23, 93).

Some brethren on the West Coast have started a paper called *The Bible Forum,* which they say is "dedicated to the open discussion of Bible subjects." It either had a short life or is way behind schedule, for I have received only three copies, the last being November 1977. All three copies are devoted to a discussion of marriage and the truth J.T. Smith and H.E. Phillips have taught. The "editorial staff" consisted of Bob Melear, Kenneth Cheatham, and Glen Lovelady. Glen Lovelady in his debate with J.T. Smith charged that the exception of Matthew 19:9 is "an addition" to the word of God, and is "what the copyist added" (*Smith-Lovelady Debate*, 176-177). Also, in this debate Lovelady raised the question of whether "the latter part of Matthew 19:9 is considered by the translators to be an interpolation of copyists" (23). By his implication, he casts doubt upon the genuineness of the text. This is what nearly all of us who have debated Baptist preachers have run into with them on Mark 16:9-20. True, some manuscripts do not contain the latter part of Matthew 19:9, but then there are probably just as many that do. The translators believed there was sufficient evidence to include it. The whole point of this is to get away from what Jesus said.

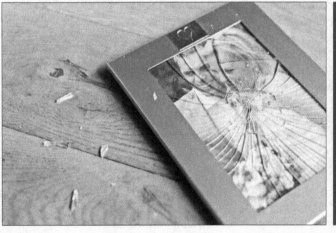

Olan Hicks has recently published a book called *What the Bible Says about Marriage, Divorce, and Remarriage*, which should be called "What Hicks Says about Marriage, Divorce, and Remarriage," for it does not teach what the Scriptures say. Hicks charges brethren who teach the truth on Matthew 19:9 with the "need to remove the glasses which have been provided for us by the Catholic Church" (26) and that the truth we teach "comes from the Vatican, not from the apostles" (29). He charges brethren with teaching "tradition" and not the Bible.

Whether they are willing to admit it or not, these men are giving comfort to the idea that the put-away fornicator can remarry without committing sin.

Definition

What is fornication? Vine defines it as "illicit sexual intercourse" and says that "it stands for, or includes adultery" (Vol. 2, 125). Thayer says, "of illicit sexual intercourse in general . . . used of adultery" (532).

What is adultery? Vine says it "denotes one who has unlawful intercourse with the spouse of another" (Vol. 1, 32-33). Thayer defines it as "to have unlawful intercourse with another's wife, to commit adultery with" (417).

Webster defines "illicit" as "not permitted; improper, unlawful" (413). For a thing to be unlawful implies the existence of a law somewhere with which one has not complied. Now, what is the law that says sexual intercourse with one to whom he is not married is sinful? It is *God's law*, for man's law says such is neither illicit nor unlawful.

Fornication is a general term including all unlawful sexual activity. Lesbianism and homosexuality would be included here as well as adultery. Adultery is a more specific term, used in reference to unlawful sexual contact with the husband or wife of another.

New Testament Teaching

In view of what men are teaching, we need to look at New Testament teaching, and a good way to do that is to look at some specific passages.

1. Matthew 5.32. Beginning in verse 31, Jesus said, "It hath been said, whosoever shall put away his wife, let him give her a writing of divorcement; But I say unto you, that whosoever shall put away his wife, saving for the cause of fornication, causeth her to commit adultery: and whosoever shall marry her that is divorced committeth adultery." Here Jesus said the man that puts away his wife causes her to commit adultery unless he puts her away for fornication. The one who marries her who is put away commits adultery. That is not "the traditional view" or what some preacher said; that is what Jesus said.

2. Mark 10:11-12. In this passage Jesus said, "Whosoever shall put away his wife, and marry another, committeth adultery against her. And if a woman shall put away her husband, and be married to another, she committeth adultery."

> All of the cases of Mary leaving Ed to marry John, even with the approval of the preacher and the elders, will not change what Christ said.

God's law given to man "from the beginning of the creation," when "God made them male and female," said, "For this cause shall a man leave his father and mother, and cleave to his wife; and they twain shall be one flesh so then they are no more twain, but one flesh. What therefore God hath joined together, let not man put asunder" (vv. 6-9). God's law, even before the church and before the law of Moses, was for "a man" to "cleave to his wife." When this was done no longer were they "twain, but one flesh." "God hath joined them together." God joins a man—someone who has left mother and father—to his wife. This passage does not teach that God joins a man who up and leaves his wife, to another woman to be his wife. Jesus said the man who puts away his wife is guilty of a sinful action, and the marrying of another is a sinful action, but it is not until he has sexual relations with her that he commits adultery. He has no right to her; it is unlawful for him to have her and every time they cohabit they commit adultery. The first act is adultery and the last one, even if twenty-five or fifty years later, is still adultery. Time does not change the unlawful to the lawful.

If a woman puts away her husband and marries another, she commits adultery. That is not the teaching of Catholicism or the traditional "Church of Christ view"; that is what Jesus said. All of the cases of Mary leaving Ed to marry John, even with the approval of the preacher and the elders, will not change what Christ said. God will not change His will just because Hicks, Lovelady, and others are teaching error, any more than he will because a Baptist preacher is teaching error.

3. Matthew 14:3-4. Matthew records, "For Herod had laid hold on John, and bound him, and put him in prison for Herodias' sake, his brother Philip's wife. For John said unto him, It is not lawful for thee to have her." Observe that Herod "had" a woman by the name of Herodias, but she was not his wife. He "had" his brother's wife. He "had" Philip's wife. John said what Herod had done was not lawful. According to whose law? Here is one who is not subject to the law of Christ, for the gospel of Christ had not yet been preached, yet he was not acting according to the law. God's law said Herodias was Philip's wife, but Herod "had" her. Herod "had" her, but God still had her joined to Philip. This shows God does not loose a wife just because man does. The court can say Mary is no longer Ed's wife and can marry John, but *God did not say that*.

4. Luke 16.18. Jesus said, "Whosoever putteth away his wife, and marrieth another, committeth adultery: and whosoever marrieth her that is put away from her husband committeth adultery." It is plain from this passage that Jesus said he who puts away his wife and marries another commits adultery. All of the human wisdom of earth will not explain it away. Then Jesus said that the man who marries the put-away woman commits adultery. Jesus said the man who puts away his wife commits adultery when he marries another, and the woman commits adultery when she marries again. Thus, four people commit adultery. That is what Jesus said.

5. Romans 7:2-3. By the Holy Spirit Paul wrote, "For the woman which hath an husband is bound by the law to her husband so long as he liveth; but if the husband be dead, she is free from the law of her husband. So then if, while her husband liveth, she be married to another man, she shall be called an adulteress: but if her husband be dead, she is free from the law; so that she is no adulteress, though she be married to another man." Paul said a woman with a husband "*is bound* . . . to her husband so long as he liveth." The way "she is loosed from the law of her husband" is "if her husband be dead." If her husband is not dead, she is not loosed from

him; she is still bound to him. If she is married to another while her husband is alive "she shall be called an adulteress." The expression "shall be called" in this verse is from the Greek *chrematizo* and is also used in Acts 11:26, where the text says that "the disciples were called Christians first at Antioch." This word means to be divinely called. God called the disciples "Christians" and God calls a woman who is married to another man while her husband liveth an "adulteress." From this passage we learn that a woman can be "married" to another man while having a husband. It should be obvious that the term "married" is not used in the sense of being married in the sight of God or that God has joined these two together when at least one of them already has a mate.

6. Matthew 19:9. Jesus said, "I say unto you whosoever shall put away his wife except it be for fornication, and shall marry another, committeth adultery; and whoso marrieth her which is put away doth commit adultery."

I have waited until this point in the lesson to introduce this passage. Previous passages noted state the general law of marriage "from the beginning." However, this passage states the "exception" given by Jesus. True, it is the only passage that says "except for fornication," but if Jesus said it once, it is the truth. Are we willing to do away with everything taught just one time in the Bible?

Christ said that "whosoever shall put away his wife . . . and shall marry another, committeth adultery." The exception Jesus gave was where the putting away was "for fornication." If one puts away a wife, but not "for fornication," or if one puts away a wife "for fornication," Jesus said, "Whoso marrieth her which is put away doth committ adultery."

NOTES

_____
_____
_____
_____
_____
_____

Questions

Matching (Match the quote with the source).

_____ 1. Matthew "inserted that exception on his own."

_____ 2. "Matthew 19:9 is considered by the translators to be an interpolation of copyists."

_____ 3. We "need to remove the glasses which have been provided for us by the Catholic Church."

_____ 4. Fornication is "illicit sexual intercourse."

_____ 5. Adultery is "to have unlawful intercourse with another's wife."

_____ 6. "Illicit" means "not permitted; improper, unlawful."

A. Lovelady

B. Garrett

C. Thayer

D. Hicks

E. Webster

F. Vine

Where's the Verse?

1. "I say unto you whosoever shall put away his wife except it be for fornication, and shall marry another, committeth adultery; and whoso marrieth her which is put away doth commit adultery."

   _____

2. "And if a woman shall put away her husband, and be married to another, she committeth adultery."

   _____

3. "For John said unto him, It is not lawful for thee to have her." _____

4. "So then if, while her husband liveth, she be married to another man, she shall be called an adulteress." _____

5. "What therefore God hath joined together, let not man put asunder." _____

What Would You Advise?

1. You have been studying the Bible with a friend for a number of weeks. You find out that he is married to a second wife. The friend requests to be baptized. What would you do? _____

   _____

2. A lady who is a Christian is deserted by her unbelieving husband. He gets a divorce, but not for fornication. You hear she is planning to remarry. You go to speak with her about her situation. She says that since her unbelieving husband left her that she is not bound to him, according to 1 Corinthians 7:15. What would you say to her? _____

   _____

3. A young wife comes to you complaining that her husband is a drunken bum who beats her. She wants to get a divorce. What advice would you give her? _____

   _____

   _____

Living in Adultery

J.T. Smith

In order for us to have a clear understanding of the subject, we need to define the word "adultery" and find out from the Scriptures what conditions constitute an adulterous situation and how one may "live in adultery."

The word "adultery" is from the Greek word *moicheuo,* and its basic meaning is "to have unlawful intercourse with another's wife, to commit adultery with" (*Thayer's Greek-English Lexicon,* 417). However, in the Old Testament, the word "adultery" was used to describe every kind of illicit sexual act, as the word was used in "Thou shalt not commit adultery," in the Ten Commandments law. According to *Young's Analytical Concordance* (368), the word "fornication" is used only five times (Ezek. 16:15, 26, 29; 2 Chron. 21:11; Isa. 23:17) in the Old Testament. In every one of these cases, the word was used to describe a spiritual condition.

> Jesus plainly points out that if one puts away (divorces) his spouse for any reason other than fornication and marries another, he commits adultery.

Unless we are going to take the position that a single man cannot look upon a single woman to lust after her and commit adultery with her in his heart, we are forced to the conclusion that the word "adultery" is used in the New Testament to describe those who are unmarried as well as those who are married. Jesus said in Matthew 5:28, "But I say unto you, that whosoever looketh on a woman to lust after her hath committed adultery with her already in his heart." Also, in 2 Peter 2:14 Peter said, "Having eyes full of adultery, and that cannot cease from sin. . . ."

In an effort to answer this argument, one of the respondents in a discussion I had on the West Coast took the position that "the definition of a word determines the meaning, not its usage in the context." I will allow you, the readers, to determine whether or not this person's conclusion is valid.

There are a number of passages I would like for us to consider in our discussion of this subject. In Matthew 5:32 Jesus said, "But I say unto you, that whosoever shall put away his wife, saving for the cause of fornication, causeth her to commit adultery: and whosoever shall marry her that is divorced committeth adultery." Again, "And I say unto you, Whosoever shall put away his wife, except it be for fornication, and shall marry another, committeth adultery; and whoso marrieth her which is put away doth commit adultery" (Matt. 19:9). Then in Mark 10:11-12 we read, "And he said unto them, Whosoever shall put away his wife, and marry another, committeth adultery against her. And if a woman shall put away her husband, and be married to another, she committeth adultery." Finally, in Luke 16:18 Jesus' statement is recorded, "Whosoever putteth away his wife, and marrieth another, committeth adultery: and whosoever marrieth her that is put away from her husband committeth adultery."

In all of these passages, Jesus plainly points out that if one puts away (divorces) his spouse for any reason other than fornication and marries another, he commits adultery. And the one who marries the "put-away one" (whether she is "put away" for fornication, a word which includes every kind of illicit sexual act, or for some other reason) commits adultery.

Another passage of Scripture that I would like for us to consider that mentions one being in adultery is Romans 7:2-3. Paul said, "For the woman which hath an husband is bound by the law to her husband so long as he liveth; but if

the husband be dead, she is loosed from the law of her husband. So then if, while her husband liveth she be married to another man, she shall be called an adulteress: but if her husband be dead, she is free from that law; so that she is no adulteress, though she be married to another man."

The word translated "commits adultery" is a present active indicative word in the Greek language that describes *continuous action*. Thus, since Jesus allows freedom from the "marriage bond" with the right to remarry for only two reasons (fornication, Matt. 19:9; death, Rom. 7:2-3), then anyone who divorces and remarries for any other reason "commits adultery." And as we noted above, this is not just a "one-time act." It involves continuous action. Every opponent whom I have met in debate on the subject of divorce and remarriage freely admits that those who divorce, without the cause of fornication being involved in the divorce are nothing more than "legalized adulterers" when they remarry.

In commenting on the expression "called an adulteress" in Romans 7:2-3, Moses E. Lard said, "To render it, as in the E.V., 'she shall be called an adulteress' is without warrant. The apostle does not mean to tell what the woman shall be called, but what business she is in. She will act the adulteress." Hence, as long as she

continues to commit the act of adultery, she is living in that condition.

Sometimes the question arises, "Why would the guilty party, the one put away for fornication, commit adultery when she remarries? Isn't the marriage bond broken when adultery is committed and one is put away for fornication—thus the guilty party loosed also? If so, the guilty party would not be 'living in adultery' when she remarried." Although this human reasoning may sound good, there are a number of things wrong with it.

In the first place, the word "marry" is being equated with the word "bound." But they are not equal. The word "bound" is from the Greek word *dedesai* and means, "to bind by a legal or moral tie, as marriage, Romans 7:2; 1 Corinthians 7:27, 39" (*Bagster's Analytical Greek Lexicon*, 89). One can be bound and not married, or he can be married and not bound. Herod's case is an example of one being "married" (according to the laws of the land) but not "bound" by God (Mark 6:17-18). In Romans 7:2-3, we find an example of one who was "married" to another but was still "bound" to her first husband. Thus, according to the above definitions, the antithesis of "bound" is "loosed," and the antithesis of "married" is "divorced." Therefore, I can tell a person who has "put away" his mate for the cause of fornication that the Lord has "loosed" him so that he is free to remarry without committing sin. However, Christ nowhere indicates that the wife is released from "her obligation" to the law of her husband.

Christ's teaching in Matthew 19:5-9 points out that there is both an "obligation" to "leave father and mother and cleave unto his wife" and both are "restricted" from having any sexual relations with anyone else. Thus the one who is put away for fornication is loosed from the obligation of "leaving and cleaving," but is not released from the restriction forbidding sexual relations with another. If so, where is the passage that shows that release? I know she is released from the leaving and cleaving to the one to whom she was married, for the Lord granted him, because of her fornication, the right to remarry. Thus their mutual agreement to "leave and cleave" is dissolved by God with the God-given right of the one doing the putting away to have a wife.

Again someone may ask, "What about 1 Corinthians 7:27-28, which says, 'Art thou loosed from a wife? seek not a wife. But and if thou marry, thou hast not sinned! Who are those who are loosed?" Yes, Paul said those who are "loosed" may be married. But who is loosed? The one who has never been married, or one whom

God, not man, has loosed. As we have already noted, God only looses the one who puts his (her) spouse away for fornication and the one whose spouse has died. All others are "loosed" by man and not by God, and if they marry they sin.

In Colossians 3:5-7 we read, "Mortify therefore your members which are upon the earth; fornication uncleanness, inordinate affection, evil concupiscence, and covetousness, which is idolatry: For which things' sake the wrath of God cometh on the children of disobedience: in which ye also walked some time, when ye lived in them." The word "fornication" in verse 5 is the general word for illicit sexual acts, and, when used by itself in a context, would include adultery. Thus, we learn from the above passages that anyone, whether alien sinner or Christian, can "live in adultery." To deny this is to deny what the apostle said. Who, then, is willing to do it?

NOTES

_____
_____
_____
_____
_____
_____

Questions

True or False

_____ 1. The word "adultery" in the Old Testament means to have unlawful intercourse with another's wife.

_____ 2. The word "fornication" in the Old Testament is never used in a spiritual sense.

_____ 3. It is possible to commit adultery in one's heart.

_____ 4. The definition of a word determines the meaning, not its usage in the context.

_____ 5. Fornication breaks the marriage bond.

_____ 6. "Fornication" in Matthew 19:9 is used only of two married people.

_____ 7. The present active indicative in the Greek language describes continuous action.

_____ 8. Jesus gave the right to remarry for only one reason.

Fill in the Blanks

1. _____ said, "The apostle does not mean to tell what the woman shall be called, but what business she is in. She will act the adulteress."

2. The word _____ means to "bind by a legal or moral tie."

3. When one marries he is to leave _____ and _____ and cleave unto his_____ .

4. "Art thou _____ from a wife? seek not a _____ ."

5. Only _____ can loose, not man.

6. "Mortify therefore your members, which are upon the earth; fornication . . . when ye _____ in them."

7. Fornication in Colossians 3:5 includes _____ .

8. Anyone, whether _____ _____ or _____ , can "live in adultery."

Discussion

1. What is the significance of the Greek tense in the phrase "commits adultery"? _____
   _____

2. Explain why the words "marry" and "bound" are not equal. _____
   _____
   _____

3. After reading Colossians 3:5-7, explain how one might be living in uncleanness, inordinate affection, evil concupiscence, covetousness, or fornication. _____
   _____
   _____
   _____

The Abortion Crisis

Bob Buchanon

The weeping prophet, Jeremiah, asked, "Is it nothing to you, all ye that pass by?" (Lam. 1:12) The Lord's people and the Lord's cause were in a sad condition indeed when these touching words were uttered. Jerusalem was sacred to the devout Jew, but when the prophet asked this question, many cared but little as to what had happened to their beloved city. The appeal of Jerusalem, not only to her neighbors, but even to the strangers passing by, was such that should have excited the compassion even of those unconnected with her. However, like our Lord's parable of the Good Samaritan, many "passed by on the other side." The same attitude of indifference, apathy, and lack of concern appears to be prevalent in our day relative to such moral issues as abortion.

On January 22, 1973, nine men robed in black ruled on abortion, striking down state laws against it. On that day the Supreme Court ruled that: during the first three months of pregnancy the decision to abort rests solely with the woman and her doctor; during the second three months, the State can regulate the abortion procedure to protect maternal health; during the third three months, when the fetus is viable, the State can regulate or even prohibit abortion except when it is necessary for the mother's mental or physical health.[1]

More and more, as laws are changed, Christians will have to consider principles in God's word to determine right from wrong.

This we have done in matters such as liquor, gambling, homosexuality, divorce, and the use of drugs; we must now do it with abortion. Although abortion has become legal, it will never become moral. To kill before or after birth is murder.

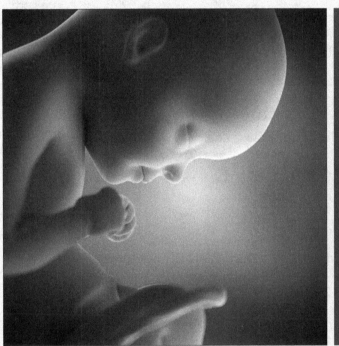

Startling Statistics

A Roman Catholic Cardinal, pleading for the "Right to Life Amendment," said: "Every nine days, there are as many deaths by abortion as there were in the entire ten years of the Vietnam War."[2]

Dr. Bernard Nathanson, the former director of New York's first abortion clinic, is convinced that he supervised the taking of 60,000 lives.[3]

---

[1] *U.S. News and World Report*, March 4, 1974, 44.

[2] CBS T.V. News, March 7, 1974.

[3] Charles and Bonnie Remsberg, "Second Thoughts on Abortion from the Doctor Who Led the Crusade for It," *Good Housekeeping*, March, 1976, 132.

It was stated in Chicago, "One out of every three children conceived will be aborted here this year. . . . An estimated 200 abortions will be performed each day in Chicago."[4]

In 1974, about 900,000 abortions were performed in the United States. The rate in Russia is about ten times higher or about 10 million abortions per year.[5]

We could continue with statistics, but figures become obsolete about as fast as the ink dries on the paper. These should suffice, however, to show us the growing problem that we face. But how concerned are you? As one brother said: "Humans tend to turn their faces away from unpleasant scenes. It is easy to prefer to stay ignorant on such issues as this. But ignorance will not excuse us, brethren. The information is available. The very land itself cries out that something must be done."[6]

The Question of Life

The whole abortion debate comes down to one question: When does the life of a separate human being begin? This question strikes at the very heart of the issue.

It was George Orwell who pointed out that it is possible to distort language so that words take on the reverse of their actual meaning. As we examine this question, we must beware of pro-abortionist terminology. To the average person, "terminate" does not mean the same as to kill, and "fetus" definitely no longer falls on the listening ear as "human," but rather as "non-human glob."[7] The abortionists may refer to abortion as simply a process of limiting fertility. He may refer to it as killing the cells and tissues of conception.[8] He may even refer to the early stages of development as "potential life."[9] We

> It is easy to get the world to approve killing a "fetus," but much less so to the killing of an "unborn baby."

must show that this is not merely "potential life," but it actually is life—human life.

"Termination of pregnancy," and "interruption of pregnancy," "retroactive contraception" all are verbal gymnastics behind which to hide the real message of what is happening. "Induced abortion" is more accurate. "Killing the life within the mother," "killing the fetus," and more to the point, "killing the unborn baby" directly face the issue, and are the most honest and preferable terms to use.[10] If you are convinced that this is a human life, call it such. We should speak of "he" or "she," not "it," and speak of the "unborn," "pre-born," or "developing child," or "baby." It is easy to get the world to approve killing a "fetus," but much less so to the killing of an "unborn baby."[11]

Development of the Baby

Basic to the consideration of whether this life within the mother is human or even when this life becomes human must be the presently known scientific facts of the development within the uterus. What are the facts concerning the development of the baby? What do we know?

In the October 1971 term of the Supreme Court, a distinguished group of 220 physicians, professors, and fellows of the American College of Obstetrics and Gynecology submitted a brief to the court. In this brief, they tried to show how modern science established that the unborn child

---

[4] *The Daily News,* Feb. 28, 1973.

[5] "Abortion Routine for Woman in Soviet Union," *The Houston Chronicle*, October 21, 1976.

[6] John Waddey, "Abortion in the Light of God's Law," *Living Soberly, Righteously, and Godly* (Lectureship of the East Tennessee School of Preaching and Mission, Knoxville, 1977) 28.

[7] Dr. and Mrs. J.C. Willke, *Handbook on Abortion* (Cincinnati, 1975) 197.

[8] C. Everett Koop, *The Right to Live, The Right to Die* (Wheaton, 1976) 31.

[9] Kenneth A. Lee, "Does the Fetus Have Any Rights?" *Christianity Applied*, November, 1974, 15.

[10] Willke, op. cit., 198.

[11] Ibid.

from the moment of conception is a person and therefore, like the mother, a patient. John M. Langone has summarized this brief. I give here several quotes from this article that pertain to the development of the child from conception through three months:

> From conception, when the sperm and egg unite, the child is a complex, dynamic, rapidly growing organism.
>
> About seven to nine days after conception, when there are already several hundred cells of the new individual formed, contact with the uterus is made, and implantation and nourishment begin. Blood cells form at 17 days, and a heart as early as 18 days. The heart starts, irregular pulsating at 24 days and about a week later smooths into rhythmic contractions.
>
> At about 18 days, the development of the nervous system is under way, the baby's eyes begin to form at 19 days, and by the 20th day the foundation of the child's brain, spinal cord and entire nervous system are established.
>
> By the 33rd day, the cerebral cortex (that part of the central nervous system that governs motor activity as well as intellect) may be seen.
>
> By the beginning of the second month, the unborn child looks distinctly human, yet the mother is not aware that she is pregnant.
>
> Brain waves have been noted at 43 days, the heart beats strongly, the stomach produces digestive juices, the liver manufactures blood cells and the kidneys are functioning.
>
> After the eighth week, no further original organs will form—everything that is already present will be found in the full-term baby. From this point until adulthood, when full growth is achieved somewhere between 25 and 27 years, the changes in the body will be mainly in dimension.
>
> In the third month, the child becomes very active and by the end of the month kicks his legs, turns his feet, moves his thumbs, bends his wrists, turns his head, frowns, squints, and opens his mouth.[12]

In spite of these facts, some people act as though the unborn child is not a human being. They are willing to cut it apart and throw the pieces into the nearest garbage can.

Dr. R.F.R. Gardner, a consultant obstetrician and gynecologist, expressed his view that the unborn child was not a human being in these words: "When a spontaneous miscarriage occurs parents may grieve, but we do not feel that we have lost a child. From time to time obstetricians have the distress of delivering a stillborn baby. We may have felt this fetus kick under our examining hands, we may have listened to its heartbeat repeatedly over four months, yet when the tragedy occurs we do not feel, 'Here is a child who died,' but rather, 'Here is a fetus which so nearly made it.' Miscarriages are not buried, are not named. . . ."[13]

> **Some people act as though the unborn child is not a human being. They are willing to cut it apart and throw the pieces into the nearest garbage can.**

Looking at Scriptures

One can take a concordance and never find where abortion is mentioned specifically by name in either testament. Is it therefore approved by the silence of the Scriptures? Many things are determined to be right or wrong by comparing them with general principles of truth as set forth in God's word. I am convinced that there are numerous divine principles that speak to this issue. Let us notice some of them.

In Exodus 21:22-24, we read: "If men strive, and hurt a woman with child, so that her fruit depart from her, and yet no mischief follow: he shall be surely punished, according as the woman's husband will lay upon him; and he shall pay as the judges determine. And if any mischief follow, then thou shalt give life for life, eye for eye, tooth for tooth, hand for hand, foot for foot." On these verses, some have argued, "If the baby is killed, only a fine is imposed; if the mother is killed, capital punishment is given. Therefore, unborn babies are not persons." But there is an

---

[12] "Abortion: The Medical Evidence Against," as quoted by Clifford Bajema, *Abortion and the Meaning of Personhood* (Baker, Grand Rapids) 25-27.

[13] R.F.R. Gardner, *Abortion: The Personal Dilemma* (Eerdmans, Grand Rapids, 1972) 126.

alternative. The words, "and yet no harm follows" may mean the child is miscarried but does not die. Then the expression, "if any harm follows" means that if the child, the mother, or both die, then the guilty party is to be capitally punished. "If men strove and thrust against a woman with child, who had come near to between them for the purpose of making peace, so that her children come out (come into the world), and no injury was done either to the woman or the child that was born, a pecuniary compensation was to be paid, such as the husband of the woman laid upon him. . . . A fine is imposed, because even if no injury had been done to the woman and the fruit of her womb, such a blow might have endangered life."[14]

Job asked, "Why died I not from the womb? Why did I not give up the ghost when I came out of the belly?" (Job 3:11) He could not "give up" what he did not have. And yet he argues that had he so died, he would have been "at rest with kings and counsellors of the earth" (vv. 13-14). If he had been "as an hidden untimely birth" (miscarriage), he would have been where "the weary be at rest" (vv. 16-17). In the tenth chapter, Job continued by wishing he had "given up the ghost, and no eye had seen (him)." But again, one cannot give up what he does not have. He would have been carried from the womb to the grave (Job 10:18-19).

While Jacob and Esau were in Rebekah's womb, they were living children. Genesis 25:22 says that "the children struggled together within her." Notice that they were called "children" while they were still in the mother's womb. This clear language shows that the life in the body of a woman is a child; it is a human being. From the time of fertilization until death, one is always a human being.

Whether in the womb or in the crib, the child is dependent. Before delivery and after delivery, he is an innocent, dependent human being.[15]

The Bible does not distinguish between prenatal and postnatal life. God said to Jeremiah,

"Before I formed thee in the belly I knew thee; and before thou camest forth out of the womb I sanctified thee, and I ordained thee a prophet unto the nations" (Jer. 1:5). The psalmist considered that the Lord watched over his development in his mother's womb (Ps. 139:13-16). Already there was a plan for his life.

Unborn John the Baptist leaped in his mother's womb when the expecting mother of our Lord greeted Elizabeth (Luke 1:41, 44). The term used to describe the baby in the womb (Greek *brephos*) is used interchangeably for "babes" before and after birth (see Luke 2:12, 16; 18:15; Acts 7:19). The word "denotes an unborn child, . . . a newborn child, or an infant still older."[16] Elizabeth was inspired by the Spirit to correctly interpret this fetal movement.

God's word has always taught, "Thou shalt not kill" (Rom. 13:9). The literal translation is "Thou shalt do no murder." Murder is the deliberate taking of innocent human life without just cause. Abortion is the planned, intentional killing of a human life. So far as I can determine, abortion is nothing more than licensed murder!

Sexual Immorality

Since abortions are now available to all minor women without parental advice or consent (Supreme Court decision, July 1, 1976), much of the "fear of pregnancy" that used to prevent a significant amount of teenage sexual immorality has been removed. The result has been an alarming increase in teenage pregnancies. Many areas are already experiencing more abortions than live births. According to a recent report, three out of ten babies born in the U.S. are illegitimate.[17]

What Can We Do?

The most constructive thing we can do is continue to instruct our young people in true moral values and Christian principles, including wholesome sex education. Many abortions are the result of conception due to fornication or

---

[14] C.F. Keil and F. Delitzch, *Biblical Commentary on the Old Testament, The Pentateuch*, Vol. II (Eerdmans, Grand Rapids, 1971) 134-135.

[15] Bob Felker, "Abortion Is Murder," *Gospel Anchor*, Vol. 3, 282.

[16] W.E. Vine, *An Expository Dictionary of New Testament Words* (Revell, Westwood, 1966) 93.

[17] *The Montgomery Advertiser*, September 24, 1978, as quoted by Ray Dutton, "The Abortion Crisis," *Christian Family*, December 1978, 7.

adultery. Paul simply states, "Flee fornication" (1 Cor. 6:18). This will avoid many abortions.

Let us be ready, however, to lend a helping hand to scared girls who find themselves pregnant out of wedlock. Other alternatives besides abortion are open to them. Certainly, adoption should be preferred over abortion; I would be one of the first on the list willing to adopt the child.

Conclusion

Yes, abortion is the killing of human life. It is wrong; it is immoral. Those guilty of murder are included in the list of those who "shall have their part in the lake which burneth with fire and brimstone" (Rev. 21:8). Let us, as God's children, rise up in holy indignation and drive this evil and sin from our midst. Let us take up the word of the Lord and dare to dream the impossible dream that some way, somehow, someday we might win our noble fight to save the innocent babes whose lives are today in jeopardy.

Questions

Multiple Choice

_____ 1. In (a. 1973, b. 1978, c. 1983) the Supreme Court struck down state laws against abortion.

_____ 2. Every (a. year, b. three months, c. nine days) there are as many deaths by abortion as there were in the entire ten years of the Vietnam War.

_____ 3. In (a. Atlanta, b. Boston, c. Chicago) one out of every three children conceived will be aborted.

_____ 4. A term that abortionists do not use to describe abortion is (a. termination of pregnancy, b. murder, c. retroactive contraception).

_____ 5. The heart forms as early as (a. 18, b. 24, c. 36) days in a pre-born baby.

_____ 6. By the (a. 20th, b. 30th, c. 40th) day the foundation of the child's brain, spinal cord, and entire nervous system is established.

_____ 7. After the (a. 7th, b. 8th, c. 9th) week, no further organs will form.

_____ 8. Since the Supreme Court decision allowing abortions for minors without parental consent, there has been (a. a decrease, b. an increase) in teenage pregnancies.

Where's the Verse?

1. "Is it nothing to you, all ye that pass by?" _____

2. "The children struggled together within her." _____

NOTES _____
_____
_____
_____
_____
_____

3. "Before thou comest forth out of the womb I sanctified thee, and I ordained thee a prophet unto the nations." _____

4. "For thou hast possessed my reins: thou hast covered me in my mother's womb." _____

5. "For, lo, as soon as the voice of thy salutation sounded in mine ears, the babe leaped in my womb for joy." _____

6. "Flee fornication." _____

7. "But the fearful, and unbelieving, and the abominable, and murderers, and whoremongers, and sorcerers, and idolaters, and all liars, shall have their part in the lake which burneth with fire and brimstone: which is the second death."

_____

_____

What Would You Advise?

1. You and a friend are talking. She reveals she is planning to get an abortion. When you ask why, she replies, "It's my body. I have the right to do what I please with it." What would be your reply?

_____

_____

2. In a class discussion on abortion, some are defending this practice by appealing to: (1) women who have been raped and would be mentally affected by having the child; (2) cases of known abnormalities in the fetus, such as mental retardation; and (3) Exod. 21:22-24, saying that the man who caused the miscarriage was only fined if the infant died. How would you answer each of these arguments? _____

_____

_____

_____

_____

3. A close friend who is a Christian comes to you for advice. She is expecting a child but knows abortion is wrong. She is seeking some possible ways to handle her unwanted pregnancy. What would you suggest? _____

_____

_____

_____

Pornography

Dennis C. Abernathy

In this chapter we shall not deal with a huge list of "statistics" and draw from that tabulation the conclusion that we have a problem with pornography! Really, all one has to do is live in our society to know that we face a grave danger in the form of pornography. Pornography is not always something with which people indulge themselves in secret (or it is not a thing done in a corner) in today's world!

Today we hear a great deal about pollution—the polluting of the air, water, the land, etc. We are in trouble! If we can believe the experts, man has so befouled his environment that now he is faced with a self-induced calamity. The pollution of the air we breathe, the water we drink, and the land we live upon is a most sinister threat to our health and happiness, and we had better be concerned about it! Former President Nixon warned: "We have become victims of our own technological genius."

But while the world's best minds grapple with the problem of air and water pollution, a far more lethal type of adulteration has descended upon us. And, ironically, this contamination arouses only slight concern compared to that of our physical environment! We are talking about "inner pollution," or pollution of the heart and mind.

Consider the man who puts up a beautiful fence around his yard, yet his yard looks like a garbage dump, or the man who beautifies the outside of his house, yet the inside is a wreck. Yet, what about the individual who wages the fight against air and water pollution, yet all kinds of filth and defilements are found lodging in his heart?

From a moral standpoint, our country has reached the "open sewer" stage. Anyone who would argue the point needs only investigate the average newsstand or glance at the entertainment pages of the local newspaper.

To read reports from those who have made a thorough investigation and appraisal of the "adults only" books, movies, etc. is shocking indeed. Even more shocking than that is the fact that this form of contamination is accelerating at an unbelievable pace. It seems that the adult movies, plays, books, etc. are competing with each other to see just how far they can go! One

New York critic, after seeing an off-Broadway play, wrote: "After this, what can there be for an encore?"

With the onslaught of this form of corruption has come a burgeoning rate of crime which is now almost beyond anyone's power to stop or even check. I wonder what our beloved America will be like when my little girls are adults!

The printed page, movies (in theaters and on television), and much of the music of today have a tremendous influence on the attitudes, manners, and morals of their recipients.

Just here I think it would be good to give a definition of pornography. *Porneia* is the Greek term for sexual uncleanness of all kinds, including fornication. *Grapho* means "to write or picture." By pornography we mean obscene books and films sold in the adult bookstore. The term includes many of the adult magazines found in the drugstores and on the newsstands. Many of the movies in the theatre and an increasing number of shows piped into our homes via TV are pornographic.

In the case of the printed page, censorship, for all practical purposes, is nonexistent. The most lurid and obscene literature imaginable is now freely circulated, obviously protected by the nation's highest courts. Listen! We are speaking about hard-core pornography, not just the "girlie magazines." It is hard to realize how lewd and vicious some of this trash really is.

> **If a man fills his heart with corruption, it will be that which flows out of his heart.**

Although these publications carry the "Adults Only" warning, any thinking person knows this is only a ridiculous attempt to justify their existence. Where is the evidence that adults are not demoralized by these publications (any person with any knowledge at all knows he is affected regardless of age)? And of course all control is lost the moment the purchase is made. There are no laws to keep such materials out of the hands of young people once they are sold. If you do not believe teenagers and even preteens are reading this obscene material, you'd better wake up. I am told (and I believe it) some of the photographs in these publications are too vile to describe—and most are of young people.

To the person whose mind is obsessed with sex, who knows little about history (and cares even less), or whose god is the "almighty dollar," the moral decline of our nation means little. Yet any sensible, right-thinking person knows that obscene literature, movies, TV, etc., encouraged by permissive courts, can fatally weaken our nation! This fact is not only underscored by history; it is affirmed by the conduct of those who have abandoned the morals of the past. Today we are witnessing a callous indifference toward patriotism and a total lack of respect for our right heritage and toward God Almighty and His Holy Word! Some of the young people today

solve their problems by painting daisies on car doors and by carrying their "Make Love, Not War" placards, etc. These are the fruits of an inner pollution problem: a pollution, I might add, that we cannot survive. "For as a man thinketh in his heart, so is he" (Prov. 23:7).

The Source of the Worst Pollution is the Human Heart

Jesus said, "There is nothing from without a man, that entering into him can defile him: but the things which come out of him, those are they that defile the man" (Mark 7:15). He then goes on in verse 18 to say: "Do ye not perceive, that whatsoever thing from without entereth into the man, it cannot defile him; because it entereth not into his heart, but into the belly, and goeth out into the draught, purging all meats? And he said, That which cometh out of the man, that defileth the man. For from within, out of the heart of men, proceed evil thoughts, adulteries, fornications, murders, thefts, covetousness, wickedness, deceit, lasciviousness, an evil eye, blasphemy, pride, foolishness: all those evil things come from within and defile the man." My dear reader, the Lord is saying that one's conduct (speech, dress, etc.) is but an evaluation of his heart. "For out of the abundance of the heart the mouth speaketh. A good man out of the good treasure of the heart bringeth forth good things: and an evil man out of evil treasure bringeth forth evil things" (Matt. 12:34-35). In other words, if a man fills his heart with corruption, it will be that which flows out of his heart. That is why the Bible says, "Keep thy heart with all diligence, for out of it are the issues of life" (Prov. 4:23).

This is the point of attack made by pornography. It affects one's heart or mind. It warps one's concept of what is right and good. It awakens, kindles, and inflames the vilest forms of lust, which lead the individual down the road of degradation and ruin. Note the following illustration:

A teen boy stops by a drugstore for a snack before going home. As he passes the magazine rack he notices a section of magazines displaying nude and seminude women. He stops and begins to shuffle the sports magazines, but his eyes are concentrated on the pornography. Passions he hasn't known before begin to stir within his mind. His curiosity is aroused, but he hesitates to reach for any of the alluring magazines. Something seems to warn him of the evil before him. For the moment, he refuses to go so far as to pick up one of the pieces of trash, but he has become careless. He has allowed pictures to lodge in his mind which have appealed to lust.

This carelessness continues for several days until one afternoon, at the same magazine rack, the boy gets bolder, bold enough to not care who is looking, bold enough to get one of the magazines in hand and look through it closely. Eventually, he has scanned the pages of all the nude magazines. The figures are fixed in his mind. He thinks about them at school. He thinks about them on a date as he makes advances to the girl. He talks about them with his buddies. He feeds his thought processes on them, as every female he sees becomes the object of hidden lust. He is bolder, now having stifled any warning of danger.

Boldness leads to habit. The boy's collection of pornography grows as he manages from various sources to buy the foul print. He is introduced to all types of sexual experiences. Through the literature he becomes acquainted with perversion in all its vile forms. Thoughts are not enough. He constantly seeks companions to fulfill his lust. On and on it goes until things happen he never imagined when he first started the downward trail. His mind is a moral sewer. His body is a diseased wreck. His future is dark. He is a slave to the lust he only played with at first!

When people ignore what God's word says about purity of heart—when they leave God out of their lives—they are on the road to ruin. Hear what Paul wrote to the Romans: "Therefore, God gave them over in the lusts of their hearts to impurity, that their bodies might be dishonored among them . . . God gave them over to degrading passions; for their women exchanged the natural function for that which is unnatural, and in the same way also the men abandoned the natural function of the woman and burned in their desire toward one another, men with men committing indecent acts and receiving in their own persons the due penalty of their error. And just as they did not see fit to acknowledge God any longer, God gave them over to a depraved mind, to do those things which are not proper . . . and, although they know the ordinance of God, that those who practice such

things are worthy of death, they not only do the same, but also give hearty approval to those who practice them" (Rom. 1:24-32).

Philipians 4:8

"Finally, brethren, whatever is true, whatever is honorable, whatever is right, whatever is pure, whatever is lovely, whatever is of good repute, if there is any excellence, and if anything worthy of praise, let your mind dwell on these things." How can one obey this injunction of Paul while filling his mind with pornography (whether it be in the form of dirty books and pictures, in the theaters or on the TV, or through the dirty and suggestive lyrics of many of the songs today)? We must cultivate proper and pure thinking and leave no room in our hearts for that which is base and vile.

Young people, heed the danger flag before you dabble with pornography. There is nothing good that can come from it. Do not be deceived. There is too much good and wholesome literature and too many good and wholesome things God has given us for us to degrade ourselves with the trash and filth coming from depraved minds. "Keep thyself pure" (1 Tim. 5:22).

If you are a sinner, purify your heart (Acts 15:9; 1 Cor. 6:11; 1 Pet. 1:22); it is through obedience to the faith (the gospel) that one's heart is purified. Have you obeyed God? Have you had your sins washed away (Acts 22:16)? Why not resolve to do that today?

Are you a Christian, who has gone back into the world (the mud and mire—the pollution of sin)? It is a low state indeed (2 Pet. 2:20-22; 2 Pet. 1:4). You need to repent of your sins and seek forgiveness at the hand of God (Acts 8:22; Jas. 5:19-20).

This is the way for the Christian, under God, to combat moral pollution in his own life. We must start with ourselves. We as parents must educate our children against the dread disease of pornography. What do your children read? What do they watch? What records do they listen to? Do you know? Do you care?

We cannot cleanse the whole world. God's people have almost always been outnumbered, outvoted, outwitted, and outraged by the pollutants which have taken over the minds, morals, and wills of wicked men. But we can begin with our own households. We can teach our children the truth concerning pornography, and we can do all in our power to eliminate it from their daily activities. Also, we can confess our sins to God, and we can be sure that our own hearts are unpolluted.

Yes, the great battle is not with water and air pollution, but with those things that pollute the heart and mind of man.

Questions

Discussion

1. Why is pornography dangerous? _____

    _____

2. List some of the forms of pornography in our present society. _____

    _____

    _____

3. Why do we need to control what goes into our minds?_____

    _____

4. What are some of the fruits of pornography? _____

    _____

    _____

Matching (Match the verse with the principle it teaches):

_____ 1. We are what we think.   A. 1 Timothy 5:22

_____ 2. We should keep our hearts with all diligence.   B. 2 Peter 2:20-22

_____ 3. We should keep our minds on wholesome things.   C. Proverbs 23:7

_____ 4. We should keep ourselves pure.   D. Proverbs 4:23

_____ 5. We should not return to the filth of the world.   E. Philippians 4:8

Agree or Disagree

1. "To ban pornographic material would take away our freedom of speech. So, censorship is against the Constitution."_____

    _____

2. "Pornographic materials lead to crimes such as child abuse, rape, homosexuality, etc."_____

3. "There is really nothing too bad about PG- and R-rated movies. They just picture life as it is. Only X-rated movies are pornographic." _____

4. "Pornography is only in the mind of the beholder. What one person may consider a work of art, another may consider pornographic." _____

5. "We should take a stronger stand against pornography. One way to do so is to boycott businesses that promote it." _____

    _____

Lesson 12

Homosexuality: What Saith the Scripture?

Mark Mayberry

Introduction

Homosexuality is the sexual attraction of an individual to members of his or her own sex. Men of this orientation are called "gay," while their female counterparts are called "lesbians." The Kinsey report of 1948 concluded that 10 percent of the general population are homosexuals. While this study was flawed and the real percentages are much lower, homosexuality is a serious problem in modern society. There are fewer homosexuals in America than activists would lead us to believe, but their influence far exceeds their numbers, especially in the media, the academic world, and the arts.

Mainline Protestant churches are deeply divided over this issue, with many pushing for the full acceptance of practicing homosexuals, both in the pulpit and the pew. Sex scandals that have rocked the Catholic Church in recent years reveal a powerful and pervasive homosexual underground in the priesthood.[1] A shift away from blanket condemnation of homosexuality to tolerant understanding and acceptance can also be witnessed among the heirs of the Restoration Movement.[2]

The pro-homosexual lobby has effectively disseminated its message. The media paint a sympathetic picture, granting homosexuals victim status, while ignoring the darker side of the gay subculture. Consider the obfuscation that has occurred on the issue of AIDS. Note the ongoing redefinition of bigotry and prejudice. Observe the extension of civil rights laws and hate crime legislation to include "sexual orientation."

Today we are bombarded with the notion that homosexuality is simply an alternative lifestyle. Those who reject this premise are accused of being narrow-minded, homophobic, hate-mongering bigots. Right and wrong, good and evil, and truth and error have been turned upside down (Isa. 5:20; Prov. 17:15; Mal. 2:17).

A Violation of Biblical Teaching

Homosexual behavior stands condemned in each Bible dispensation. In the Patriarchal Age, God's disapproval of such conduct is seen in the destruction of Sodom and Gomorrah (Gen. 19:1-25).

In the Mosaic Age, the Law said: "You shall not lie with a male as one lies with a female; it is an abomination" (Lev. 18:22). Anyone who violated this prohibition was subject to execution (Lev. 20:13).

---

[1] For more information, see Michael S. Rose, *Goodbye! Good Men* (Aquinas Publishing Ltd., 2002). See also, Donald B. Cozzens, *The Changing Face of the Priesthood: A Reflection on the Priest's Crisis of Soul* (Liturgical Press, 2000).

[2] For more information, see the archives of the Stone-Campbell email Discussion List at the following URL: http:// bible.acu.edu/ministry/resources/mailinglists.html

In the Christian Age, homosexuality is condemned in the strongest terms. Romans 1 declares, "The wrath of God is revealed from heaven against all ungodliness and unrighteousness of men who suppress the truth in unrighteousness." Homosexuality and lesbianism are set forth as prime examples of darkened understanding and sinful folly. Such lifestyles are degrading, dishonorable, impure, indecent, unnatural and wholly unacceptable (Rom. 1:18-27). Unrepentant homosexuals are counted among "the unrighteous" who will not inherit the kingdom of God (1 Cor. 6:9-10). In discussing the necessity of law, Paul identifies various forms of harmful and criminal behavior that must be restricted. Murderers, kidnappers, liars, perjurers, immoral men, and homosexuals share a common disregard for what is right. Such conduct demonstrates a spirit of lawless rebellion and is contrary to sound teaching (1 Tim. 1:9-10).

Cultural accommodationists would blunt the force of these passages. "Such a clear-cut, black and white approach is too simplistic," they argue. "The issue is far more complicated. Moralistic judgments must be replaced by tolerant understanding." Evading clear and consistent scriptural teaching, they attempt to shift the focus and change the issue.

Redefining God's Message from the Patriarchal Era

Some argue that the inhabitants of Sodom and Gomorrah were condemned, not because of their homosexual lifestyles, but because they failed to practice hospitality.[3] Yet, this assertion does not harmonize with the Genesis account or inspired NT commentary on the same. According to the Sacred Text, "The men of Sodom, compassed the house round, both old and young, all the people from every quarter: And they called unto Lot, and said unto him, Where are the men which came in to thee this night? Bring them out unto us, that we may know them" (Gen. 19:4-5). Did they just want to become acquainted? Socialize? If so, then this interpretation negates the charge of being inhospitable. No, Sodom was a sex-drenched society; the problem of perversion was pervasive. Homosexual predators came from all age groups ("young and old") and every social strata ("all the people from every quarter"). They attacked Lot's house, seeking to "know," i.e., have carnal relations with, his angelic visitors. Recounting various examples of divine judgment, Peter said the destruction of Sodom and Gomorrah was a warning to those who would thereafter live "ungodly lives." Lot was "oppressed by the sensual conduct of unprincipled men," his righteous soul being tormented day after day by their "lawless deeds." God's power and providence are evident: "The Lord knows how to rescue the godly from temptation, and to keep the unrighteous under punishment for the day of judgment, especially those who indulge the flesh in its corrupt desires and despise authority" (2 Pet. 2:6-10). Jude says the inhabitants of Sodom and Gomorrah indulged in "gross immorality" and went after "strange flesh." Accordingly, they are set forth as an example of those who will undergo the punishment of eternal fire (Jude 7).

Redefining God's Message from the Mosaic Era

Others would weaken the force of the Levitical prohibitions, saying that the real issue is idolatry, as opposed to sexual orientation. For example, *The New Bible Dictionary* says,

> The force of the other OT references to homosexuality is similarly limited by the context in which they are set. Historically, homosexual behaviour was linked with idolatrous cult prostitution (1 Kings 14:24; 15:12; 22:46). The stern warnings of the Levitical law (Leviticus 18:22; 20:13) are primarily aimed at idolatry too; the word "abomination," for example, which features in both these references, is a religious term often used for idolatrous practices. Viewed strictly within their context, then, these OT condemnations apply to homosexual activity conducted in the course of idolatry, but not necessarily more widely than that.[4]

---

[3] For more information, see Derrick Sherwin Bailey, *Homosexuality and the Western Christian Tradition* (London/New York: Longmans, Green, 1955). See also Daniel A. Helminiak & John S. Spong, *What the Bible Really Says about Homosexuality* (Alamo Square Press, 1994).

[4] D.R.W. Wood, ed., *New Bible Dictionary,* 3rd ed. (Leicester, England; Downers Grove, IL: InterVarsity Press, 1996), 478-479.

Yes, Canaanite fertility cults encouraged full and free sexual expression. Heterosexuality, homosexuality, and harlotry (male and female) were all feverishly practiced in the worship of idols. Yet, certain questions must be asked: Was homosexuality judged sinful because of its association with idolatry, or did it fall under independent condemnation? What about other

> **The Modernist View of Scriptural Ethics: Whenever New Testament teaching conflicts with politically correct views of the modern world, especially as it relates to marriage, the roles of men and women, sexual orientation and behavior, etc., it is automatically assumed that biblical authors are unenlightened, bigoted brutes.**

forms of sexual expression: adultery, fornication, pedophilia, incest, or bestiality? Were they morally neutral, except when associated with idol worship? Are we merely speaking of guilt by association? No. All the aforementioned practices violate the divine pattern of sexual purity. From the beginning, God has intended that one man be joined to one woman in marriage for life (Gen. 2:24; Matt. 19:3-9). Physical longing finds proper expression only within the relationship of marriage (Prov. 5:15-19). Within a God-ordained, divinely-recognized relationship, marriage is honorable and the bed undefiled; outside such boundaries, all sexual activity is counted as evil (Heb. 13:4).

As Merrill F. Unger said, "Fertility cults nowhere controlled people more completely than in Canaan. When Israel entered Palestine, the Canaanites were in the last stages of degradation as the result of centuries of worshiping degrading deities. The only safe recourse for the Israelites was complete separation and annihilation of the Canaanites and their religion. Orgiastic nature worship, fertility cults in the form of serpent symbols, unbounded license, and moral abandon could only be met with a severe code of ethics."[5]

Pagan idolatry was not one wrong action (image worship) incidentally coupled with other actions that were morally neutral (homosexuality). Rather, it involved the piling up of sinful deeds: idolatry, sexual debauchery, human sacrifice, etc. Individually and collectively, such deeds were judged by God as an abomination.

The Hebrew word *toebah* (Strong #8441) frequently occurs in the Old Testament. In the NASV it is translated "abominable" (5x), "abominable act" (lx), "abomination" (39x), "abominations" (60x), "detestable" (2x), "detestable act" (lx), "detestable thing" (3x), "detestable things" (3x), "loathsome" (2x), "object of loathing" (lx). *Strong's Enhanced Lexicon* defines it as "a disgusting thing, abomination, abominable." In the "ritual sense," it referred to unclean food, idols, and mixed marriages. In the "ethical sense," it identified base wickedness.[6] Swanson says it describes a "detestable thing, abomination, repulsion, i.e., an object which is loathsome and abhorrent. The object may be a concrete 'thing' or a 'way' or 'practice,' as lifestyle behavior."[7]

Discussing the various nuances of this word, R. Laird Harris says, "As with the verb, so also with the noun the abomination may be of a physical, ritual or ethical nature and may be abhorred by God or man. Sharing a meal with a Hebrew was ritually offensive to an Egyptian (Gen. 43:32), as was offering certain kinds *of* sacrifices (Exod. 8:26). Homosexuality and other perversions are repugnant to God and fall under His judgment (Lev. 18:22-30; 20:13). Idolatry (Deut. 7:25), human sacrifice (Deut. 12:31), eating ritually unclean animals (Deut.

---

[5] Merrill F. Unger, ed. R.K. Harrison, *The New Unger's Bible Dictionary, Revised & Updated Edition* (Chicago: Moody Press, 1988), s.v. "Idolatry: Canaan."

[6] James Strong, *Enhanced Strong's Lexicon* (Ontario: Woodside Bible Fellowship, 1996), s.v. "H8441."

[7] James Swanson, *Dictionary of Biblical Languages with Semantic Domains: Hebrew Old Testament* (Oak Harbor: Logos Research Systems, Inc., 1997), s.v. "HGK9359."

14:3-8), sacrificing defective animals (Deut. 17:1), conducting one's business dishonestly (Deut. 25:13-16), practicing ritual prostitution (1 Kings 14:23f), and similar acts *of* disobedience (for seven more abominations, see the list in Proverbs 6:16-19) were sure to bring God's wrath on those who perpetrated them."[8]

Redefining God's Message from the Christian Era

Many reject the aforementioned teaching in Romans, 1 Corinthians, and 1 Timothy by saying that Paul merely echoes the anti-homosexual bias of his strict Jewish upbringing. John Spong, Episcopal Bishop of Newark, New Jersey, dismissed the apostle Paul as a "self-loathing and repressed gay male." Such statements are so outrageous they deserve no response. Nevertheless, they reflect a widely-held approach to Scripture: Whenever New Testament teaching conflicts with politically correct views of the modern world, especially as it relates to marriage, the roles of men and women, sexual orientation and behavior, etc., it is automatically assumed that biblical authors are unenlightened, bigoted brutes.

Yet, such an approach denies both the inspiration and authority of Scripture. Jesus promised to send the Holy Spirit to guide the apostles unto all truth (John 14:25-26; 16:13-15). With the outpouring of the Spirit on the Day of Pentecost, this promise became reality (Acts 2:4). Later, Paul affirmed the inspired nature of his message (1 Cor. 2:9-13).

Because of their divine origin, the Holy Scriptures are profitable for teaching, reproof, correction and training in righteousness (2 Tim. 3:16-17). However, for truth to remain truth, it must be accepted in its entirety: "*All* Scripture inspired of God is profitable. . . ." Man is not permitted to pick and choose which biblical truths he deems acceptable and reject the rest. Divine truth forms a harmonious whole. Thus, the repeated warning: Do not add to, subtract from, or alter the word of God (Deut. 4:2; 12:32;

Prov. 30:6; Gal. 1:6-9; Rev. 22:18-19). Any addition to the true knowledge of God makes it something other than truth (2 Pet. 1:3). Any subtraction from the perfect law of liberty renders it less than perfect (Jas. 1:25).

> We live in just such a confused culture: children are out of control; women rule the roost; real men are rarely seen. Is it any wonder, then, that homosexuality flourishes in such an environment?

A Violation of Biblical Purity

Homosexuality clearly violates the New Testament prohibition against *porneia* (fornication, sexual immorality, unchastity), *akatharsia* (uncleanness, impurity), and *aselgeia* (lasciviousness, licentiousness, sensuality, wantonness). These Greek words condemn all sexual activity outside of marriage, whether heterosexual or homosexual (Gal. 5:19-21; Eph. 4:17-24; 5:3-12).

Homosexuality is also addressed by two additional Greek words: *malakos* and *arsenokoites,* which appear together in 1 Corinthians 6:9-10. Many commentators and translators understand these terms as references to passive and active partners in male homosexual intercourse.[9]

Arsenokoites is a combination of *arsen,* translated "male, men" and *koite,* translated "bed" (Luke 11:7; Heb. 13:4), "conceived" (Rom. 9:10), or "sexual promiscuity" (Rom. 13:13), and therefore identifies "an abuser of (one's) self with mankind, homosexuals, sodomites" (1 Cor. 6:9; 1 Tim. 1:10). Strong defines *arsenokoites* as "one who lies with a male as with a female, sodomite,

---

[8] R. Laird Harris, *Theological Wordbook of the Old Testament* (Chicago: Moody Press, 1999, c 1980), 977.

[9] Geoffrey W Bromiley, ed. *The International Standard Bible Encyclopedia* (Grand Rapids: Wm. B. Eerdmans, cl979-1988; Logos Research Systems: 2001), s.v. "Homosexuality."

homosexual."[10] Swanson says it refers to a "male homosexual, one who takes the active male role in homosexual intercourse."[11]

Malakos can refer to either soft, fine clothing (Matt. 11:8; Luke 7:25) or men who are soft and effeminate (1 Cor. 6:9). Strong says it is used metaphorically, in a bad sense: effeminate; of a catamite; of a boy kept for homosexual relations with a man; of a male who submits his body to unnatural lewdness; of a male prostitute."[12] Arndt and Gingrich say it is used "of persons soft, effeminate, esp. of catamites, men and boys who allow themselves to be misused homosexually."[13] Louw and Nida say the word identifies "the passive male partner in homosexual intercourse."[14]

The point needs to be made that the Bible sets forth distinctive roles for men and women (Eph. 5:25-3; Titus 2:4-5; 1 Tim. 2:11-15; 1 Pet. 3:1-7). In action, dress, and demeanor, God wants men to be men and women to be women (Deut. 22:5; 1 Cor. 11:3-16). Men ought not to be soft; women ought not to be overbearing. Men need to cultivate the characteristics of manliness, and women, the qualities of femininity. Fathers need to teach their sons courage, conviction, compassion, and a strong handshake. Mothers need to teach their daughters to be meek, quiet, and submissive. However, note that trouble occurs when God's pattern for home and family life is ignored (Isa. 3:9-12). We live in just such a confused culture: children are out of control; women rule the roost; and real men are rarely seen. Is it any wonder, then, that homosexuality flourishes in such an environment?

A Violation of Biblical Order

Because the Gentiles refused to acknowledge God, remember His will, honor His name, or give thanks for His many blessings, God gave them over to degrading lusts. Exchanging the natural function for what is unnatural, they dishonored their bodies among themselves, practicing lesbianism and homosexuality (Rom. 1:21-27). What can be learned from this description of homosexual behavior?

First, it is perverse. Paul describes homosexual conduct as impure, indecent, dishonorable, and degrading. The inhabitants of Sodom and Gomorrah engaged in brazen behavior (Isa. 3:9-12) and indulged in gross immorality (Jude 7). *Ekporneuo,* translated "gross immorality," is an intensified form of *porneuo.* In other words, homosexuality is an excessive form of sexual depravity, involving conduct that is utterly unchaste and wholly immoral. Such shameful behavior is inconsistent with the honorable position held by mankind (Gen. 1:26-28; Ps. 8:3-8).

Second, it is a choice. They *exchanged* the truth of God for a lie, and worshiped and served the creature rather than the Creator (v. 25). They *exchanged* the natural function for that which is unnatural (v. 26). The Greek word translated "exchanged" means "to change, exchange, barter away, cease and start, one activity for another." In other words, homosexuality is not determined by genetics, but is an active choice made by free moral agents. We choose either to obey the will of God or rebel against his commandments (Gen. 4:6-7; Deut. 30:15-20; Josh. 24:14-15; Rom. 6:16-18).

Third, it is unnatural. Women exchanged the natural function for that which is unnatural (v. 26). Men abandoned the natural function of the woman and burned in their desire toward one another (v. 27). Nature teaches a distinction between men and women (1 Cor. 11:14-15). Nature teaches an attraction between men and women (Eph. 5:31). Sexual relations between a man and woman accord with nature; such relations between members of the same sex

---

[10] James Strong, *Enhanced Strong's Lexicon* (Ontario: Woodside Bible Fellowship, 1996), s.v. "#733."

[11] James Swanson, *Dictionary of Biblical Languages with Semantic Domains: Greek New Testament* (Oak Harbor: Logos Research Systems, Inc., 1997), s.v. "#780."

[12] James Strong, *Enhanced Strong's Lexicon* (Ontario: Woodside Bible Fellowship, 1996), s.v. "#3120."

[13] Walter Bauer, William F. Arndt, F. Wilbur Gingrich, & Frederick W. Danker, *A Greek-English Lexicon of the New Testament and Other Early Christian Literature,* 2nd ed. (Chicago: University of Chicago Press, c1979, Logos Research Systems: 1996), 488.

[14] Johannes P. Louw, *Greek-English Lexicon of the New Testament: Based on Semantic Domains* (New York: United Bible Societies, c1989, 1996), s.v. "88.280-281."

conflicts with the same. The inhabitants of Sodom and Gomorrah went after strange flesh. In other words, they followed a path that was different (Greek: *heteros)* from God's established order (Jude 7). Homosexuality differs from God's pattern of heterosexuality.

Fourth, it is driven by insatiable lust. Abandoning the natural function of the woman, men burned in their desire toward one another (v. 27). The word translated "burned" means "to kindle, to set on fire, to inflame deeply." As indicated by the derivation of the Greek word *arsenokoites,* sexual perversion grows out of an inordinate focus on the bed and all that it represents. Instead of being satisfied with God's pattern of monogamy—one man, one woman, for life—the sensualist seeks new and diverse thrills. In this regard, the homosexual who deifies sex is much like the drug addict. The latter requires an ever greater dosage to achieve the same high. The former requires an ever more perverse form of sexuality to achieve the same thrill.

As the KJV says, "evil men and seducers shall wax worse and worse, deceiving, and being deceived" (2 Tim. 3:13). Moral standards continue to degenerate. With each passing year, perversion reaches new depths. The 1948 Kinsey Report provided the intellectual foundation for advancement of the "gay rights" agenda in the latter half of the twentieth century. Fifty years later, in the media, universities, and professional organizations, there is a concerted, broad based push for acceptance of pedophilia

as an alternative lifestyle.[15] What deviancy will next appear on the ever expanding sexual frontier? What will the future hold for our children and grandchildren?

> The Holy Scriptures offer no support to the notion that homosexuality is a morally acceptable alternative lifestyle.

Conclusion

The Holy Scriptures offer no support to the notion that homosexuality is a morally acceptable alternative lifestyle. Instead, the Bible identifies homosexual activity as a sin, even as it does heterosexual activity outside of a God-sanctified marriage.

Yet, hope is extended to all men. Concluding his categorization of soul-condemning sins, Paul said, "Such were some of you; but you were washed, but you were sanctified, but you were justified in the name of the Lord Jesus Christ and in the Spirit of our God" (1 Cor. 6:11). The sin of homosexuality does not put one beyond the reach of God's saving grace. The gospel plan of salvation calls sinful humanity to faith, repentance, confession, and baptism. We must

---

[15] For more information, see Judith Levine, Foreword by Joycelyn M. Elders, *Harmful to Minors: The Perils of Protecting Children from Sex* (University of Minnesota Press, 2002). See also Bruce Rind, Philip Tromovitch, and Robert Bauserman, "A meta-analytic examination of assumed properties of child sexual abuse using college samples," *Psychological Bulletin,* 1998, 124, 22-53. Additional information is available through The Leadership Council, 191 Presidential Boulevard, Suite C-132, Bala Cynwyd, PA 19004, http://www.leadershipcouncil.org.

NOTES

_____

_____

_____

_____

_____

_____

hear God's word and believe it, especially as it speaks to our sins and transgressions. We must repent, i.e., change our thinking and our conduct. Dying to the old man of sin, we are buried with Christ in baptism, wherein we contact the cleansing power of His blood, and are raised to walk in newness of life (Rom. 6:1-7).

Questions

1. How is the issue of homosexuality affecting the Protestant and Catholic religions?_____

_____

_____

2. How are homosexuals treated in the mainstream media? _____

_____

3. What does the Bible say about those who turn the truth upside down? How does this apply to the current discussion? _____

_____

_____

4. How do cultural accommodationists discount biblical teaching on the subject of homosexuality?

_____

_____

5. What does the term "know" mean in Genesis 19:5?_____

_____

6. What abiding lessons are taught by God's overthrow of Sodom and Gomorrah? _____

_____

_____

7. List the various practices identified in the OT as "an abomination." _____

_____

_____

8. Are the aforementioned acts reckoned as evil because of their association with idolatry, or are they individually condemned?_____

9. Refute the following assertion: "When Paul addresses the subject of homosexuality, he reflects, not the will of God, but his own bias and bigotry."_____

10. Can we pick and choose among biblical truths, accepting some and rejecting the rest? _____

11. How is a repudiation of a portion of Scripture, in fact, a denial of the whole of Scripture? _____

_____

12. How does homosexuality violate God's standard of purity? _____

_____

13. How does modern culture blur the distinction between the sexes? _____
_____

14. What are the characteristics of true masculinity? _____
_____

15. What are the characteristics of true femininity? _____
_____

16. Explain how homosexuality is debasing. _____
_____

17. Is homosexuality genetically predetermined or is it a lifestyle choice? _____

18. Discuss the similarity between homosexuality and drug addiction. _____
_____
_____

19. Provide examples of modern society's continued moral degeneration. _____
_____
_____

20. What hope is extended to homosexuals? On what basis can sinners obtain forgiveness? _____
_____
_____

Dancing

Marshall E. Patton

Dancing is an age-old problem in the church, and it continues to present itself anew with each rising generation. While the problem appears over and over, dancing itself appears in a new form from generation to generation. This study shows, however, that the same basic evil in dancing of the past is likewise present in that of the current generation—hence, the problem, regardless of the form or the generation.

Objectivity

One aspect of the problem is found in the fact that far too many do not study the issue objectively. All too often social, sometimes a party spirit, and other pressures make for a prejudiced, biased, and opinionated study. Some hold that preachers are so bound by antiquated views, tradition, and a desire for acceptance among their peers that their teaching is void of objectivity and that because of these pressures they simply cannot "get with it" in this modern hour. Bible class teachers are sometimes viewed in much the same light, and others who oppose dancing are thought of by some as radicals, "killjoys," and objectors without due regard for facts.

In the hope of greater objectivity, let it be observed that while the possibility of such on the part of some exists, surely more serious thought shows such views to be a reflection upon the integrity of our teachers in general, as well as a threat to our future security. Those who are experienced, who are void of a reputation of extremism, and who are recognized as careful students of the word are well-schooled in the dangers of such pressures influences. Among these, we find many who have the faith and courage to search out and stand for truth, regardless of such influences and consequences. The consensus judgment of such is worthy of the greatest respect and study.

Consensus Judgment

I believe that it goes without debate that the consensus judgment of the most faithful among us (preachers, elders, deacons, Bible class teachers, and others) is that dancing, as opposed in this article, is wrong. It would be folly for one seriously ill physically to ignore the consensus judgment of the best qualified in the realm of therapeutics. Likewise, we must conclude that it would be equally foolish to ignore the consensus judgment of the best qualified in the field of Bible knowledge. Young people especially should be very careful to avoid the path of folly in their study of this issue.

Inconsistency

Inconsistency poses a problem for both the guilty and the observer. All of our literature that is used in Bible classes, religious papers, tracts, books of sermons, etc. that deals with this subject sounds a unanimous voice against dancing. The Christian, therefore, who engages in such finds himself at variance with the literature throughout the brotherhood, as well as the oral teaching thereof. This puts him in a bad light with his fellows and at a disadvantage to explain his inconsistency to others.

Dancing in the Bible

The dancing of which one reads in the Bible may be divided twofold: (1) There were dances expressive of great joy and gratitude on occasions of victory and wonderful favors wrought or bestowed at the hand of God; also, dances by which devotion, honor, and praise were shown unto Him (e.g., Exod. 15:20; Judg. 11:34; 1 Sam. 18:6; 2 Sam. 6:14; Psa. 30:11; 149:3; 150:4; Luke 15:25). In these dances men and women danced alone—no mixed dancing. (2) There were dances for amusement, pleasure and entertainment. These often involved hilarity, revelling, and mixed dancing (e.g., Exod. 32:19-

28; 1 Sam. 30:16; Job 21:7, 11-20; Matt. 14:3-6; Mark 6:21-28). Concerning the two kinds of dancing, only the former has any semblance of approval by God. Even then, those involving some religious aspect (praise unto God) are found in the Old Testament. There is no authority for such in the New Testament age (John 4:23, 24).

Works of the Flesh

Among the works of the flesh (Gal. 5:19-21), we find "lasciviousness." Webster defines this word as follows: "wanton, lewd, lustful—tending to produce lewd emotions; the synonym of licentious, lecherous, salacious—the antonym of chaste." Again, it is defined: "indecent bodily movements, unchaste handling of males and females" (*Thayer's Greek Lexicon*, 79, 80). There are two expressions in the definitions worthy of special attention, because they identify, beyond doubt, the modern popular dance styles (as well as others), namely, "tending to produce lewd emotions" and "indecent bodily movements." The suggestive positions, provocative movements, and seductive gyrations of modern dance styles are here identified as lasciviousness.

If one were trying to produce lewd emotions by indecent movements of the body, could he do better than employ the bodily movements of such dances? In order to see more clearly the lascivious aspect, omit for the moment the presence of music and ask the question, "Is there a Christian woman anywhere who would condone another woman engaging in such bodily movements before her husband—even in her own living room?" The presence or absence of music does not change the lascivious aspect. One thing wrong with dancing is that it takes and grants privileges that are not tolerated anywhere else in decent society. Even if a mature Christian (one schooled and experienced in the control of his passions) should be able to withstand temptation, we need to remember that the average man of the world is void of such strength, and many could not care less.

Sometimes women say that such does not so affect them. Perhaps there are exceptions—more often among teenaged and single young women. This point involves a study of the psychological and biological differences between the male and female, which space limitations forbid just now. However, just remember that no matter how innocent one may be of lewd emotions in such dances, he cannot be sure that such does not "produce" or "tend to produce lewd emotions" in another. Remember, "lasciviousness" is condemned in the words, "They which do such things shall not inherit the kingdom of God."

"Revellings" is also listed among the works of the flesh. A study of this word as defined by Webster and by lexicographers shows that it means a lack of restraint and self-control; emotional excitement; and that which is boisterous, loud and noisy. While this word may not be descriptive of every form of dancing that falls into the category of amusement, pleasure, and entertainment, it is descriptive of the modern dance club and all that is associated therewith. It, therefore, must be considered in a study of this theme.

A few years ago, Paul Harvey, under the heading of "Pagan Dance Nothing New," said:

> I had no business in that night club except that friends insisted I "should know what's going on."
>
> It was one of those places where, in suspended cages, girls wiggle and giggle to a jungle drum beat. Later, I'm told, they dance on tabletops among the customers. I didn't wait.
>
> Anyway, I said, "that's one degree of vulgarity that I'll never get on TV!" . . .
>
> Choreographers must never have read anything more profound than *Billboard* and *Playboy* if they genuinely consider their product avant garde. It is, conversely, as old as the Old Testament and as unimaginative as burlesque.
>
> The Greeks, the Romans, the Persians, the Egyptians, the Arabs, the Turks, the Sardinians, the Mongolians, the Chinese—certain alley cats and dissolute dogs—long ago allowed such self expression as is masqueraded as "new" (Paul Harvey, ABC News, Via *Bedford Bulletin*, Vol. 1, No. 52, Jan. 16, 1966).

According to an AP dispatch from Hollywood (some time ago), Ginger Rogers said of the dance called the "twist":

> The twist is ungraceful, vulgar, and exhibitionism personified. I think it's scandal. It is the most obscene dance I've ever seen, worse than the shimmy ever was (Via *God Speaks to Today's Teenagers*, by James Meadows).

Space limitations preclude further quotations which show that even many who are "not of us" put those who engage in such dancing in a bad light. This is significant in relation to the issue because of the principle of influence (Matt. 5:16).

It should also be observed that in listing the works of the flesh, Paul adds to "lasciviousness" and "revellings" the expression "and such like." These works of the flesh identify acts that would excite unlawful desires and passions on the part of either the performer or observer. Furthermore, it does not meet the issue to say that properly supervised and sponsored dancing falls into a different category. Supervision can have some control over the aspect of revelry, but one cannot supervise the thoughts, emotions, and passions of another.

Dancing, as opposed in this article, identifies the participant as foolish, inconsistent, indulging the works of the flesh, condemned by the Scriptures, and without hope of heaven. Repentance is mandatory by a loving Heavenly Father, who would have all men to be saved.

NOTES

_____
_____
_____
_____
_____
_____

Questions

True or False

_____ 1. Dancing is just a recent problem.

_____ 2. Most mature Christians believe dancing is wrong.

_____ 3. The Bible approves of some types of dancing.

_____ 4. Webster defines lasciviousness as "indecent bodily movements."

_____ 5. Dancing causes some to be aroused sexually.

_____ 6. Ginger Rogers said square dancing was "the most obscene dance she had ever seen."

_____ 7. Dancing will not harm one's influence.

_____ 8. One who has engaged in mixed dancing should repent.

What's Wrong with These Excuses?

1. "Dancing is just a form of exercise." _____

   _____

2. "I can dance and control my thoughts." _____

   _____

3. "I just go to chaperoned dances." _____

   _____

4. "The Bible commends dancing." _____

   _____

5. "Anyone who thinks dancing is wrong is just old-fashioned." _____

   _____

6. "I just go to the dances; I don't actually dance." _____

   _____

Mystery Word

(Fill in the answers to the words going across in the following puzzle. If you have the correct answers, a mystery word will appear in the bold column.)

1. What one should do if he dances.
2. How we should study the subject of dancing.
3. A work of the flesh meaning wanton, lewd, lustful.
4. Where sinners will not be in eternity.

5. Where sinners will be in eternity.

6. The man who listed the works of the flesh.

7. The kind of light a Christian should be.

8. The sin studied in this lesson.

9. The one whom we should obey.

1. ☐☐☐☐☐☐

2. ☐☐☐☐☐☐☐☐☐☐

3. ☐☐☐☐☐☐☐☐☐☐☐☐☐

4. ☐☐☐☐☐☐

5. ☐ ☐☐☐

6. ☐☐☐☐

7. ☐☐☐☐☐

8. ☐☐☐☐☐

9. ☐☐☐

Lesson 14

Immodest Dress

Jefferson David Tant

Immodesty, lust, adultery, deceit, drunkenness, and murder. Not a very pleasant list of words, is it? And, some might wonder why we would put immodesty and murder in the same category. The reason is that all of the words listed belong in the same narrative and are listed in the progressive order of events, beginning with immodesty and ending with murder. You should recognize the story of David and Bathsheba from 2 Samuel 11:1-12:25.

Do women realize the power and influence they exercise over the thinking and actions of men by way of sexual attraction? Surely this is well illustrated by the sad story of Israel's great king and his beautiful neighbor. Who knows the reasons for Bathsheba's displaying herself immodestly within the view of David? But we can see that this action, however innocent it may have seemed to her, brought forth sin, sorrow, and death, and its consequences reached into the distant future for the king of Israel. From his rooftop, David was able to look upon Bathsheba while she was bathing within his view. Her beauty and lack of discretion contributed to lust within David's heart. Their resulting adultery caused a child to be conceived. To cover the sin, Bathsheba's husband, Uriah, was recalled from the battlefront, as David sought to provide opportunity for others to think that the child was by Uriah. But this loyal subject and soldier refused to go in to his wife while his comrades were on the battlefield. David then got Uriah drunk so he might go to his wife, but Uriah still refused. David finally sent a sealed message by Uriah to his captain on the battlefield, which caused Uriah to be placed where he was certain to be killed. Who would ever have thought that such a vile deed would have come from such an "innocent" beginning? But such is the way of the world—both then and now.

We truly live in an age that worships at the feet of Aphrodite, the Greek goddess of sexual love. The manifestations of this sex worship are evident and plentiful. We have an increase of "living together" arrangements, an epidemic of venereal disease, one million pregnancies among unmarried teenagers each year, a flood of pornographic literature and movies, and a vast expanse of bare skin. They all go together, and to try to determine which came first would result in a "chicken-or-egg-first" type of debate. But there may be some substance to the idea that the trend towards a more revealing style of dress in previous years has in turn created an atmosphere that has fostered a decline in moral standards everywhere.

Question: Is the Bible teaching on modest apparel relevant to this age? Yes, if we believe in an all-wise, all-powerful, and all-knowing God. Therefore, God had the ability to design laws, commandments, and principles suited to all men of all nations of all time (Matt. 24:35; 1 Pet. 1:23). Man's nature has not changed, and a reading of the Bible will reveal the same emotions, passions, and human attributes that men have today. Therefore, what God teaches through the Bible is relevant. And it is obvious that it needs to be made relevant to those who profess to be Christians today who adorn themselves in their shorts, miniskirts, swimsuits, low necklines, tight outfits, and see-through styles.

Biblical Principles Governing Dress

Nakedness has always been a symbol of shame, beginning with Adam and Eve in Genesis 3:7. The aprons they made for themselves might well have covered about as much as a modern swimsuit, but God was not satisfied with this, as He made for them "coats of skins" (Gen. 3:21) to clothe them. Nakedness was also used as a symbol of spiritual shame (Isa. 47:3; Rev. 3:18). Note that you can have clothing on and still be naked in the biblical sense. The word is used in the sense of "thinly clad" in such passages as Job 22:6 and James 2:15-16. According to this, you are "naked" in many of the modern costumes that are accepted as normal attire.

God has said, "In like manner, that women adorn themselves in modest apparel, with shamefacedness and sobriety; not with braided hair, and gold or pearls or costly raiment: but (which becometh women professing godliness) through good works" (1 Tim. 2:9-10).

"Modest" from the Greek means "well-arranged, seemly. . . ." Thus dress is to be orderly, in good taste, and in such fashion as to cause a woman to be respected, to be thought highly of. Some argue that "good taste" is reflected in whatever the current fashions are. That may be true to a certain extent, but custom can go beyond the principles of godliness, and the Christian is told to "be not fashioned according to this world: but be ye transformed by the renewing of your mind, that ye may prove what is the good and acceptable and perfect will of God" (Rom. 12:2). With this attitude, we are not so eager to ape the fashions of this world and justify ungodliness just because "everyone else is doing it."

"Shamefacedness" is "a sense of shame, modesty, reverence, the ability to blush." This is more akin to our modern use of "modesty" which is defined as "not forward; shy or reserved. Behaving according to a standard of what is proper or decorous; decent; pure; now especially, not displaying one's body" (Webster). In keeping with this definition, can one honestly defend many modern styles? To put it plainly: Girls (young or not so young), would you be embarrassed for a man to walk into your room and see you in your underwear? If you have any shamefacedness at all, your answer is "yes." Then why not show the same attribute in public and refuse to wear the shorts and halters and otherwise revealing costumes that so many try to defend? Does the fact that the name of one is "shorts" and the other is "underwear" make the difference between modesty and immodesty? Be honest with yourself!

Clothing indicative of shamefacedness is the opposite of that type which is a bold display or which is forward in nature. This rules out clothing which exposes and emphasizes the private parts of the body and which therefore tends to produce unwholesome thoughts. If you could hear some of the comments the men and boys make concerning the girls who pass by in tight outfits, shorts, low-cut blouses and the like, surely it would bring a blush. Such clothing may be considered lascivious (encouraging lewd or lustful thoughts or emotions) and is condemned as a work of the flesh in Galatians 5:19-21.

Our text in 1 Timothy also uses "sobriety," which indicates "soundness of mind, self-control" and "good judgment, moderation . . . especially as a feminine virtue, decency" (Arndt and Gingrich). Here is clothing that is moderate, kept within bounds, restrained, in keeping with good judgment.

When these unchanging principles are destroyed, immodesty results, and sin comes. But when one seeks to conform to God's standards rather than those of the world, modesty will be sought rather than shunned, and godliness will be practiced rather than worldliness defended.

The Results of Immodest Clothing

Even the world recognizes the significance of the emphasis on sex in clothing. In the first place, it tends towards exhibitionism. "The women on the beach whom the men can't help watching are . . . the ones with figures who want men to watch them and are bold enough to show this in their manner . . . But one complication is that some people have a greater-than-average urge to make the opposite sex look at them, by means of clothes or the lack of them. Certain of the people know it. Others of them don't admit it, even to themselves" ("Dr. Spock Talks with Mothers," *Ladies Home Journal*, September 1955, 26, 28). "Women no longer wince at revealing their bodies in this 'naked era,' deliberately adapting their choice for the purpose of attracting the male, and to call a spade a spade, often to get the men hot and bothered" (*Woman! The Dominant Sex,* 115). Mary Quant, the well-known fashion designer and mother of the miniskirt: "Mini-clothes are symbolic of those girls who want to seduce a man." Whether the miniskirt itself is in or out of style at any particular time is not the point. The point is that that particular garment is but one of the many products of the sexual revolution.

Another problem is that such clothing is recognized as contributory to crimes. "Some rapists, Dr. Hoffman points out, are harmless until their inhibitions are freed by drink or dope. Others however, need only the sight of a scantily clad female to trigger sexual violence. And the way some girls run around the streets today, Dr. Hoffman says, is practically asking for it . . ." ("How to Protect Your Family," *Cosmopolitan,* January 1962, 47). We could go on with page after page of similar quotes, including a comprehensive survey conducted among the Police Departments around the United States, concerning the sharp rise in sex crimes against women in the last several years. Ninety percent of the officers responding related sex crimes to immodest styles of clothing. And these officers are not the psychiatrists sitting in their ivory towers giving forth their lofty philosophies, but the men who have to deal with crime and its victims in the streets day after day. A major city's vice squad commander agreed with others that husbands and fathers have "some responsibility to uphold sensible standards" in clothing for their families, because men know more clearly what may be provocative. These officials suggested the sex crime rise might be slowed by responsible action of school officials, employers and proprietors, designers and manufacturers, entertainers, religious leaders, writers, and advertisers.

Such clothing also sends a message. In a discussion with a group of young people, the question was asked why girls (and boys) go around with shirts or blouses unbuttoned to a daring extent and wear otherwise suggestive clothing. The consensus was that it was done for advertising purposes. In the police survey, 7,601 of those responding said a girl is more likely to "involve herself in immoral behavior by the subjective effect" of wearing daring clothing. It also sends the message that they no longer care what God thinks, for if they did, they would never appear in public in clothing that is purely of, by, and for the world. They no longer care about themselves, for they have given up self-respect and care about personal safety. And they no longer care what effect they have on others, having no concern that their unchaste display may create lust in the heart of some youth who is growing into manhood, but still lacks the maturity of self-control.

Why is it that many places, including U.S. military installations around the world, prohibit the wearing of shorts and halters and like clothes in public? Why are such styles prohibited in prison? When I visited an inmate in prison recently, I was interested in the regulations concerning clothing posted in the visitors room. No shorts, no halters, no low necks, etc. Do you really have to guess at the reason? See Matthew 5:28 for a clue.

I want to share with the readers part of a letter I received from a teenaged girl after she had read something I had written on modesty.

How some of the girls I know call themselves Christians can wear the clothes they do, I just don't know. Some of them don't know better and some of them do. . . .I don't know about all of the parents, but I know some of them think their teenage girls are justified in the way they dress and act. It really bothers me that the parents and preachers and class teachers don't talk about modesty. . . . When I think of all the Christian girls I know of going around in hiphugger jeans and midriff blouses, and miniskirts or body shirts, it really bugs me." From the teenager's point of view, I'll tell you some of the arguments I've heard: (1) "The latest fashion is and I just don't want to look different." (2) "All of my friends will think I'm crazy." (3) "My boyfriend will

Do we really want to dress like, act like, and be like the world? Or do we want to "walk worthily of the calling wherewith ye were called" (Eph. 4:1)?

drop me fast if I dress like that" (modestly). (4) "No one's ever told me it was wrong." (5) "The preacher has never said a thing to me about my short dresses." (6) "My parents say it's all right, so. . . ." Do you see the main ingredient in such reasoning? It is dressing to please others rather than dressing to please God! It is seeking to be "fashioned according to this world" rather than dressing in a way "which becometh women professing godliness."

The Bible describes two types of clothing: the attire of a harlot (Prov. 7:10), and modest apparel (1 Tim. 2:9). If you honestly consider the matter, it should take no intellectual giant to figure out in which category to place the mini-clothes described by their creator as "symbolic of girls who want to seduce a man."

What this all leads to finally is just plain sin. Do we really want to dress like, act like, and be like the world? Or do we want to "walk worthily of the calling wherewith ye were called" (Eph. 4:1)? Do we not desire to be that "elect race, a royal priesthood, a holy nation, a people for God's own possession, that ye may show forth the excellencies of him who called you out of darkness into his marvellous light. . . . Beloved, I beseech you as sojourners and pilgrims, to abstain from fleshly lusts, which war against the soul; have your behavior seemly among the Gentiles; that, wherein they speak against you as evil-doers they may by your good works, which they behold, glorify God in the day of visitation" (1 Pet. 2:9-12).

When all is said and done, do we want the approval of the world or of God? The final reward of heaven or hell will depend upon our answer.

NOTES

_____

_____

_____

_____

_____

_____

Questions

Who Said It?

1. "I am with child." _____

2. "I have sinned against the Lord." _____

3. "I was afraid, because I was naked; and I hid myself." _____

4. "And be not conformed to this world." _____

5. "Mini-clothes are symbolic of those girls who want to seduce a man." _____

6. "Whosoever looketh on a woman to lust after her hath committed adultery with her already in his heart." _____

   _____

7. "There met him a woman with the attire of an harlot." _____

8. "Abstain from fleshly lusts, which war against the soul." _____

Matching

_____ 1. "Thinly-clad"   A. Lascivious

_____ 2. "Well-arranged, seemly"   B. Sobriety

_____ 3. "A sense of shame."   C. Naked

_____ 4. "Encouraging lewd or lustful thoughts or emotions."   D. Shamefacedness

_____ 5. "Soundness of mind"   E. Modest

Agree or Disagree?

1. "Immodest dress may lead to rape." _____

2. "Only women can be guilty of immodesty." _____

3. "If someone lusts at me because of my dress, that's his problem, not mine." _____

4. "Women who dress immodestly seek to draw attention to themselves." _____

5. "As long as one is dressed similarly to those around him he is modest. It is when one dresses in such a way to call attention to himself that he becomes immodest." _____

6. "Shorts are immodest." _____

7. "If my parents okay my dress, then it must be okay." _____

8. "There are two types of clothing—modest clothing and immodest clothing." _____

The Swimsuit Question

Ron Halbrook

Blatant immodesty was once limited to such haunts of unrespectable sin as houses of prostitution, bars, and nightclubs. The circus has often displayed women in costumes which "hesitated to begin and ended almost immediately," as one Kentucky preacher complained more than 100 years ago (*Apostolic Times*, 6 May 1875, 186). Nowadays, it seems that all sins have become "respectable," no sin more so than the sin of exposing the body in lascivious attire. Extremely low-cut fronts and backs on dresses have appeared in a variety of styles, one of the latest being the "disco" look. The miniskirt, after being the rage for several years, has become one among many in the smorgasbord of lascivious styles in our "do-your-own-thing" society. Shorts, halters, tubes, and swimsuits have become a way of life for many people, no more to be questioned than apple pie, mother, and the American flag. Immodest dress is treated as a human right, involving the right of men to look with pleasurable lust upon women's figures and the right of the women to entice men's pleasurable lust by displaying their figures.

Proper Attitudes and Proper Clothing

When sin broke into the world through Adam and Eve, over the protest of God, the power of sinful lusts was unleashed, cursing mankind to this day. Before sin entered, Adam and Eve had lived in fellowship with God, in marital companionship with each other and in the same innocent nakedness which is still seen among small children. Immediately upon sinning, Adam and Eve experienced shame in nakedness and made apron-like girdles to wear. God replaced these with coat-like garments (cf. Gen. 3:7, 21). Wherever mankind has gone, the bodies of men and women have been covered because of the influence of God's word, the shame of sin, and the reality of temptation. Lack of clothing has characterized cultures darkened by rejecting God, embracing sin, and delighting in pleasurable lusts.

Clothing reflects attitudes. Enticed by "the attire of an harlot," foolish men have destroyed their souls in lust and sin (Prov. 7). Once a man possessed by demons went about with "no clothes," but was healed by Jesus and was then seen "clothed, and in his right mind" (Luke 8:26-36). Godly women are *inwardly adorned* with "a meek and quiet spirit," with an awareness of the shame of sin, and with a sober attitude toward the dangers of temptations. This inner spirit of submission to God is reflected in all facets of a godly woman's life, *including the clothes she wears* (1 Pet. 3:1-7; 1 Tim. 2:9-10). She blunts, by her careful dress, the destructive powers of temptation in those who look upon her. Her dress stirs up admiration and respect rather than lascivious thought. What does the practice of men and women appearing before each other in modern swimsuits reflect, *the darkness of sin or the high standards of God's Word?*

Understand and Respect Sexual Nature

It is not wrong for a woman to be sexually attractive to a man. Indeed, God convinced Adam that no creature was suitable to his needs; then, He created woman as a companion suitable in every way. This *one* man was given *one woman*, and this one woman was presented to one man that the two might "*be one flesh*" (Gen. 2:18-24). The sexual relationship was thus a gift from God for the good of man and woman, rather than something ugly, shameful, dark, and unclean.

Our sexual capacity is a gift to be enjoyed, not an evil to be endured. The joy, steadfastness, faithfulness, and passion of love between man and woman are celebrated poetically in the Song of Solomon. "Marriage is honorable in all, and the bed undefiled: but whoremongers and adulterers God will judge" (Heb. 13:4). The beauty and purity of the bed upon which sexual love is shared can be preserved only as each partner shares that love with *the one mate alone.*

> Drink water from your own cistern,
> running water from your own well.
> should your springs overflow in the streets,
> your streams of water in the public squares?
> Let them be yours alone,
> never to be shared with strangers.
> May your fountain be blessed,
> and may you rejoice in the wife of your
>   youth.
> A loving doe, a graceful deer—
> may her breast, satisfy you always,
> may you ever be captivated by her love.
> Why be captivated, my son, by an
>   adulteress?
> Why embrace the bosom
>   of another man's wife?
>   (Prov. 5.15-20, NIV).

The very sight of the woman's body—unclothed or nearly so—stimulates sexual pleasure in the man, thus making her delightful, tantalizing, and desirable to him. It is a great blessing to find one's mate attractive and to share the sexual privileges of marital love. The sexual union, intercourse, or companionship of marriage is a part of the creation which God pronounced "very good" (Gen. 1:31). Both the personal needs and the pleasures of individuals are served, as is humanity's need for reproduction (Gen. 1:28; 2:18; 1 Cor. 7:2-4).

Satan has perverted every gift of God, including the gift of sex. Fornication, in its broadest meaning, is any sexual intercourse which violates and abuses the law of God. Satan tempts unmarried people to experience sexual union, thereby committing the sin of fornication. He tempts married people to have sexual relations with someone to whom they are not married under God's law, thus committing a form of fornication called adultery. Our adversary is smart enough to know that all sin begins in the heart (Matt. 15:16-20). Therefore, the first step

in fornication is for a man to look on a woman to whom he is not married, stirring up the desire, will, and intention for intercourse with her. Whether or not he gains the opportunity to unite his body with hers, he has "committed adultery with her already in his heart" (Matt. 5:27-28). Satan has many devices to encourage such lusts in the heart, and these devices are called lasciviousness. The lascivious spirit weakens the sense of modesty and restraint by stirring up the fires of temptation and lust. This can be done through words, dances, pictures, and dress. Much of modern society accepts lasciviousness as a way of life, a legitimate means of pleasure, and even a business tool in advertising.

Men can be tantalized by women in clothing which is arranged so as to reveal rather than

to cover the woman's body, or which is so brief as to present the body nearly unclothed. For a woman to appear this way before her husband alone, and thus to make herself attractive to him, is a privilege given to them in marriage by God. For a woman to appear this way before other men is lascivious. As pleasures and desires are stimulated in the hearts of these men, she becomes guilty of the terrible sin of causing others to sin. In this lascivious age, many men think they have the right to these sinful pleasures and desires, and many women think they have the right to "catch man's eye" by dressing so as to stir his lusts. So terrible is this sin in God's sight that Jesus said it were better for her that a millstone were hanged about her neck, and that she were drowned in the depth of the sea (Matt. 18:1-14). Jesus also said it were better for these men if they had no eyes (5:29).

Modern Swimsuits: Reflection of a Lascivious Society

Exact styles of dress are not specified in God's word; differences from nation to nation, age to age, and person to person are allowed. Still, the Christian is regulated by divine principle in dress, as in all facets of life. We may enjoy different styles and modes of dress, except when they violate the principles of God's Word. If unlimited change is permitted and God has no concern for dress at all, then nudity itself can be justified. Does the modern swimsuit (worn by a female who is sexually mature in the presence of a male to whom she is not married) *fall within the limitations of God's word, or outside those principles in the lascivious spirit of an ungodly age?*

Some who think that Christian women can appear before men in the abbreviated cloth wrapping which covers what little it covers in the form-fitting style of a sausage casing. It would be hard for these people to prove absolute nudity wrong. Yet, occasionally, some Christian conforms his or her ways so much to the ways of this age that it becomes necessary to rationalize certain practices. For instance, the danger of appearing in mixed company in swimsuits must be explained away by arguing something like this: "We can be like the world in innocent matters. Perhaps at one time people of the world were provoked to ungodly thoughts by the sight of woman in her swimsuit, but the practice is now so widely accepted that no normal person notices such a thing anymore. The practice no longer attracts attention and so has become innocent." To be around our friends of the world and to hear them speak with lascivious delight about this or that woman in a swimsuit is to know how hollow the above rationalization is. Conscientious Christian men try to avoid the situation or look away when the sight of a woman in a swimsuit presents itself, in the effort to guard the thoughts of their hearts.

On other occasions, Christians who are determined to defend such practices will concede the lascivious thought as a problem for the sinner but not for the Christian: "It is all right for *a group of Christians* to go mixed swimming in modern swimsuits because our minds are pure, and none of us would be tempted by ungodly thoughts." While it is true that Christians strive to discipline their thoughts, it is untrue that a Christian male cannot experience lascivious desires at the sight of the tightly-outlined or nearly-nude form of a female body. Baptism does not make eunuchs of men; it does not change the chemistry of male-female biology. Men do not enter the baptismal water in bodies of flesh and emerge in bodies of stone or steel. Christians discipline their thoughts, but also admit the ever-present reality of temptation and danger of sin as long as we are in the body. Remembering what happened to King David ("a man after God's own heart," Acts 13:22) when he chanced to look upon a woman's exposed body, Satan knows that he may well take advantage of the modern Christian who is so arrogant as to assert, "Now, that I'm a Christian, lascivious thoughts *cannot* be stirred in my mind and fornication can *never* seriously tempt me again." If the above rationalization has any merit, it could as well prove that a nudist colony populated by Christians alone would be all right!

The testimony of the world itself about whether swimsuits tend to stir up lascivious desires would be the most conclusive evidence possible. When the world speaks of its own things, the testimony is decisive. The funny papers, comic strips, and comedians reflect a common sense kind of psychology; they make us laugh at ourselves, at the real world. Among situations often made the brunt of a joke is the man who walks into a wall or drives his car into a telephone pole while craning his neck to see a woman exposed in shorts, a tight dress, or a swimsuit. The man's accident under such circumstances may be funny, but the reality of his lascivious thoughts and of her exposure which stirred them *is no laughing matter.* Eloquent testimony also comes from the advertising industry, which has made untold millions of dollars by knowing what attracts the attention of people. In ads for everything from sodas to cars, advertisers utilize the lascivious effects of women in swimsuits to gain audience attention on billboards, in magazines, newspapers, and on television. Is this industry convinced that normal men today *do* or *do not* take special notice of a woman whose body is exposed in a swimsuit?

The Bible teaches a woman to cover her body so that it will not be an object of lust, temptation, and lasciviousness.

Time Magazine (December 11, 1978), in the "American Scene" column, points out that what keeps many football fans from running for hot-dogs at halftime is the sight of female cheerleaders in their twirling costumes. What better way is there "to catch a man's eye" than in these costumes, which are "tight," "stretchy," and "skimpy"? The article adds that the performances reflect "dance lessons" and include attractive "struts and tosses" of the female body. In other words, people of the world freely admit that such costumes and performances are enjoyed in pleasurable lusts by men who live in an age which accepts such lasciviousness as commonplace and justifiable. Twirling costumes are based upon the same pattern as one-piece swimsuits. While the world freely admits the pleasure of looking at female bodies exposed in lascivious attire, the worldly minded in the church deny that (1) such attire is lascivious, and that (2) normal men take special notice of such attire. Brethren who make these denials are grossly ignorant (perhaps sheltered from the real world and unexposed to the realities of temptation) or are intellectually dishonest (refuse to admit the facts condemning a practice they are determined to continue).

What Shall We Do Then?

Some who once were in the world have been baptized but not converted, and so have brought the world into the church. Others who once opposed the practice of mixed bathing in lascivious swimsuits have surrendered to the increasing power of worldliness, like Gideon, who compromised the truth after having fought for it. Feeling the worldly pressures from *within* the church, they say, "If we preach on this, we will run off the members." Feeling the worldly pressures from *without*, they say, "If we preach on this we will be viewed as fanatics by the community." Forgotten in many cases is the heavenly call to preach the truth "in season and out of season" (2 Tim. 4:1-5).

Let us not surrender to the gloom! When we teach those within, the honest of heart will repent and only the hypocrites will be driven away. When those without hear stirring condemnations of sin, they will be touched by the power of the gospel, as the Spirit intended (John 16:8; Rom. 1:16). Their awareness of sin will bring them to the cross. This writer recently baptized the same hour of the night a young adult who heard one gospel sermon and who wanted to hear more afterwards because, she said, "I know what you said about swimsuits is true. I've been there—I've been guilty of the very things you warned of and know them to be true." Faithful Christians can determine to teach modesty and to oppose sinful modern swimsuits. Many are so teaching, and many elders are standing behind this teaching. Irven Lee says that a church which tolerates such worldliness as gambling, social drinking, and immodesty of mixed swimming is a "garbage church"—and every town needs a garbage dump to collect unconverted brethren who persist in worldliness so they cannot ruin good churches. Consistent teaching keeps the church pure by encouraging the strong to stay strong, helping the weak to grow, and causing the stubborn to exit in search of their own kind.

NOTES

_____

_____

_____

_____

_____

_____

Questions

Completion

1. 1 Timothy 2:9-10: "In like manner also, that women _____ themselves in _____ apparel, with _____ _____ and _____ not with _____ hair, or _____ _____ , or _____ array; But (which becometh women professing _____) with good _____ ."

2. 1 Peter 3:3-4: "Whose _____ let it not be that _____ adorning of the hair, and of_____ of _____, or of putting on of _____ ; But let it be the _____ man of the _____ , in that which is not _____, even the ornament of a _____ and _____ spirit, which is in the sight of _____ of great _____ ."

3. Matthew 5:28: "But I say unto you, That _____ looketh on a _____ to _____ after her hath committed _____ ." _____

4. Matthew 5:29: "And if thy right _____ offend thee, _____it out, and _____ from thee: for it is _____ for thee that one of thy _____ should _____ , and not that thy

   whole _____ should be cast into _____ ."

5. Matthew 18:6: "But _____ _____shall _____ one of these little ones which _____ in me, it were _____ for him that a _____ were hanged about his _____, and that he were _____ in the _____ of the _____ ."

Which Column?

(Place the following people in the proper category in the chart below).

1. Adam and Eve in their apron of leaves.

2. Adam and Eve in their coats.

3. The harlot.

4. The man possessed by demons.

5. The woman of 1 Peter 3:1-7.

6. The woman of 1 Timothy 2:9-10.

Modest	Immodest

What Would You Do?

1. A girlfriend asks you (another girl) over to a swimming party she is having for a group of girls. After you have been there for a while a group of boys crash the party and join in the swimming. All the other girls continue to swim. What would you do? _____

    _____

    _____

    _____

2. A friend says she is going to try out for the cheerleading squad. She wants you to join with her. Knowing the type of clothing that cheerleaders wear and some of the activities they are involved in, what would you do? _____

    _____

    _____

    _____

Dishonesty

S. Leonard Tyler

Dishonesty is distasteful, despicable, detested, and even hated by most people, but lies at least dormant, if not digging, within the secrets of every man's heart. Is it not characteristic of most of us to shift, squirm, imply, bypass, overlook, shun, or outright lie about certain acts, duties, feelings, or intentions? Would you not classify such as dishonest? This should impress us with the pertinence of our study. Behold, dishonesty may well lie smoldering within your own heart ready to flare up and destroy. Dishonesty, as any impurity, does not dictate every thought and act, but along life's way somewhere it sends forth its venom and the work is started.

What Is Dishonesty?

"*Dishonest* implies a willful perversion of truth in order to deceive, cheat, or defraud" (*Webster's Seventh New Collegiate Dictionary*). "The reverse of honesty; lack of probity or integrity; disposition to lie, cheat, or steal; fraud or thefts;

a dishonest act" (*The New Century Dictionary*). W.E. Vine in his *Expository Dictionary of New Testament Words* gives, "Dishonesty; *aischune* . . . shame, so the R.V. in 2 Cor. 4:2 (for A.V., 'dishonesty'), is elsewhere rendered 'shame,' Luke 14:9; Phil. 3:19; Heb. 12:2; Jude 13; Rev. 3:18" (318).

Dishonesty, to me, is an attitude or disposition of self-centeredness, and exaltation of one's own wisdom, pleasure, desire, judgment, imagination, and ambitions as the standards for life without due consideration or appreciation otherwise for right or wrong, good or evil. It is an attitude without regard to right principles or even truth itself. Oh yes, the degree of pressure or environmental circumstances determine whatever consideration is given, but not what is right or wrong, good or evil.

Too many pick up towels, linens, etc. in motels, cram expense accounts, pick up little things in stores, forget income, or overload the deductibles

on tax returns, and add to damaged cars in accidents to save the $100 deductible. I won't even mention the "not-at-home" responses when certain people appear at the door or when the phone rings. In these, we need to watch out lest we teach our children to lie. Some lie in order to climb a little higher on the social ladder (what about in business, politics, doctors' placebo pills?). Others manifest just plain pretentious false action, and on and on we could go. Our society has certainly become dishonest.

Honesty and Dishonesty Are Opposites

The wise approach to our study, it seems to me, is to look at the positive side: honesty. Since dishonesty is the opposite of honesty, one should settle his own mind as to honesty. Opposites are not definitions but antonyms—contrary in tendency, character, or meaning. A definition is "a statement of the essential nature of anything; a formal statement of the meaning or signification of a word, phrase, etc." (*The New Century Dictionary*). What is it to be honest or dishonest?

Thayer, in his *Greek-English Lexicon of the New Testament* (322), gives, "*Kalos* (prob. primarily 'sound,' 'hale,' 'whole;') . . . beautiful applied by the Greeks to everything so distinguished in form, excellence, goodness, usefulness" and "(c) beautiful by reason of purity of heart and life, and hence praiseworthy, morally good, noble. . . ." W.E. Vine in his *Expository Dictionary of New Testament Words* under "honest" lists *semnos* in Philippians 4:8 as translated in A.V. "honest" and *euschemonos* as rendered "honestly" in Romans 13:13 and 1 Thessalonians 4:12.

Therefore, an honest heart is open and receptive to truth and right and will, to the extent of its ability, properly appropriate all the knowledge with genuine sincerity to ascertain and accept the right conclusions. It is uncontaminated with selfishness, prejudicial opinions, or calloused biases and earnestly seeks to find and walk in the right ways of life.

An honest heart can be ignorantly wrong but can never knowingly continue in the wrong. An honest or dishonest heart is characterized by attitude, not knowledge; accomplishment, not right or wrong. An honest heart acts upon and within the bounds of the knowledge possessed with sincerity and confidence that such action is good and right. The understanding may be faulty, but in ignorance one acts honestly. This is following one's conscience. What one feels or thinks according to his knowledge of what is proper and right must dictate his action, if he is honest. However, his doing such does not make it right. "What makes right?" you may ask. The proper standard of established truth does. In spiritual matters, God's word, the Bible, is that standard of authority (John 12:48; 1 John 3:4; 2 John 9). Let me illustrate.

Paul Is an Example

Paul persecuted Christians; he laid waste the church of our Lord and gave consent to Stephen's death, but he was honest (Acts 8; 23:1). He thought God wanted him to do exactly what he did, i.e. "many things contrary to the name of Jesus of Nazareth" (Acts 26:9-11), notwithstanding, the fact that he was wrong. Thinking a thing to be right does not make it right, regardless of how honest one may be. Paul tells his own story in 1 Timothy 1:11-16. He said, "I was before a blasphemer, and a persecutor, and injurious; but I obtained mercy, because I did it ignorantly in unbelief." Ignorance does not justify, excuse, or make right any more than unbelief in this statement. However, if and when one acts within the bounds of his own knowledge, thinking that to be right, he acts honestly. But remember, when one learns truth, honesty demands that he accept it. Paul did that with readiness of mind and heart and fully committed himself to Jesus Christ, and the one whom he once ignorantly persecuted he now lovingly and faithfully proclaimed as both Lord and Christ (Gal. 1:13-24).

God's truth establishes what is right spiritually (2 Pet. 1:3). Jesus told those who would abide in His word, "Then are ye truly my disciples; and ye shall know the truth, and the truth shall make you free" (John 8:31-32). Paul was honest and gladly gave up all things "for the excellency of the knowledge of Christ Jesus my Lord" (Acts 22:16; Phil. 3:8).

Felix and Agrippa as Examples

Felix with his wife Drusilla heard Paul reason upon "righteousness, temperance, and judgment to come." Felix trembled, and answered, "Go thy way for this time; when I have a convenient season, I will call for thee" (Acts 24:25). He wanted money and a convenient season, but neither came. Dishonesty is deadly and unending.

Agrippa and Bernice, in great pomp, heard Paul's appeal, and Agrippa responded, "Almost thou persuadest me to be a Christian" (Acts 26:28). His heart was not open to truth, and he declined the Lord's invitation. Paul pleaded to no avail, "I would to God, that not only thou, but also all that hear me this day, were both almost, and altogether such as I am, except these bonds."

The Parable of the Sower

Jesus explains the parable of the sower who sowed seed upon different kinds of ground. (1) The wayside hearts hear but make no pretentions to obey. The devil comes and snatches the word out of the heart. (2) The rocky ground hearts hear and receive the word with joy, but, lacking root depth, fall away (dishonesty reigns). (3) The thorny ground hearts receive and go forth to be choked out with cares, riches, and pleasures of this life. These seek self-fulfillment of fleshly desires, and the word is cast aside. They love unrighteousness more than the righteousness of God (2 Thess. 2:10-12).

The good ground hearts ("the honest and good hearts") receive (believe and obey) and produce fruit with patience. These are the people who—with open eyes, ears and hearts—hear the voice of the Lord with understanding, and their lives are changed. They are converted because they received the word of the Lord (Matt. 13:18-23; Luke 8:11-15; 6:46; Jas. 1:21-25).

Dishonesty within the Ranks of the Believers

Ananias and Sapphira planned together to deceive concerning the gift of their possessions. Peter asked, "Why hath Satan filled thine heart to lie to the Holy Ghost?" (Acts 5:1-11). Here is demonstrated God's disposition toward dishonesty. We might well take notice and beware of the consequences. These fell dead.

Simon the sorcerer thought he could buy the power of God with money. Peter told him that his heart was not right with God. He responded to the reproval and asked for the apostle's prayers (Acts 8:13-24). These cases are relevant to our time of prosperity and ability to give liberally and cheerfully, without pretentious cravings or deceitful ambitions. Christians are to purpose in their hearts and give according to prosperity. What kind of hearts do we have?

All hypocritical action is dishonesty. "Let no corrupt speech proceed out of your mouth" (Eph. 4:25-32; Col. 3:8-9; 1 Pet. 2:1; Matt. 12:34). Dishonesty is too often manifested in repeated stories.

Dishonesty among Elders, Deacons, Preachers, and Teachers

Paul told the elders of Ephesus that after his departure grievous wolves would enter, not sparing the flock, "also of your own selves shall men arise, speaking perverse things, to draw away disciples after them" (Acts 20:30). False doctrine is just as damnable when taught by an elder as by a grievous wolf. It is not who teaches but what is taught. No one has the prerogative to speak for the Lord. His word is revealed. "If any man speaks, let him speak as the oracles of God" (1 Pet. 4:11).

John complimented the Ephesians for trying certain false apostles and finding them liars (Rev. 2:2). He also branded Diotrephes as dishonest because he was seeking the preeminence, "prating against us with malicious words," and would not receive faithful evangelists nor even allow others to receive them without casting them out of the church (3 John 9-10).

Peter and Jude portray dishonest teachers so vividly. Peter impresses us by saying, "There shall be false teachers among you, who privily shall bring in damnable heresies," and even deny the Lord. Jude reports that "certain men crept in unawares . . . ungodly men, turning the grace of God into lasciviousness . . . walking after their own lusts; and their mouth speaketh great swelling words, having men's persons in admiration because of advantage" (2 Pet. 2; Jude). These were ungodly and dishonest but were teaching with great swelling words. Jesus says, "All these evil things come from within, and defile the man" (Mark 7:23).

Dishonesty is a condition of heart and must be guarded against all the days of one's life. Dishonesty will destroy one's character, steal his integrity, and strip him of all worthy confidence and trust. It is truly a destructive attitude and a terrible condition of heart and will ultimately destroy the soul. No wonder Solomon said, "Keep thy heart with all diligence; for out of it are the issues of life" (Prov. 4:23). Jesus said, "How can ye, being evil, speak good things? For out of the abundance of the heart the mouth speaketh. A good man out of the good treasure of the heart bringeth forth good things; and an evil man out of the evil treasure bringeth forth evil things" (Matt. 12:34-35). Keep yourself honest before God.

Questions

Yes or No?

_____ 1. Is it possible for any of us to be guilty of dishonesty?

_____ 2. Is telling only half-truths being dishonest?

_____ 3. Could there be situations in which it doesn't pay to be honest?

_____ 4. After hearing the truth, can one remain in error and continue to be honest?

_____ 5. Is one who is doing wrong always dishonest?

_____ 6. Is it possible for us to lose the word of God after it has been planted in our hearts?

_____ 7. Can one lie to God?

_____ 8. Is it impossible for a member of the church to be unjustly cast out of the church?

_____ 9. Is the heart involved in dishonesty?

NOTES
_____
_____
_____
_____
_____
_____

Matching

_____   1. Ignorantly persecuted Christians.   A. Ananias

_____   2. Said the truth would make us free.   B. Agrippa

_____   3. Was waiting for a convenient season.   C. Peter

_____   4. Was almost persuaded to be a Christian.   D. Diotrephes

_____   5. Lied to the Holy Spirit.   E. John

_____   6. Thought he could buy the power of God with money.   F. Felix

_____   7. Said we should speak as the oracles of God.   G. Simon

_____   8. Complimented the Ephesians for finding false teachers.   H. Saul

_____   9. Would not receive faithful evangelists.   I. Jesus

What Would You Do?

1. Suppose you were living in Germany during Hitler's persecution of the Jews. Two Jews ask you to give them shelter and you do. The Nazis later come to your door asking if you are hiding the Jews. What would you do? _____

    _____

    _____

    _____

2. A salesman has come to your door. He asks if your parents are at home. But your parents have told you to tell him they are not in. What would you do?_____

    _____

    _____

3. An elder for whom you have a great deal of respect teaches something in a class you do not believe is in the Bible. When you question him privately, he says it is nothing to be concerned about. What would you do? _____

    _____

    _____

Lesson 17

Shoplifting

Jerry Parks

Did you know that the Bible says absolutely nothing about shoplifting? But the Bible has much to say about thieves, stealing, dishonesty, greed, selfishness, extortion, deception, covetousness, and crime—principles which need to be taken into consideration when discussing our modern-day term, "shoplifting." It is a crime punishable by law, as well as a sin in the sight of God. The shoplifter is a thief. He or she is stealing, dishonest, greedy, covetous, and selfish. Such a person is engaging in deception and extortion. This being the case, it is easy to see how a study on the subject of shoplifting fits into the general theme of morality.

I doubt if many of us realize the seriousness of this problem. Shoplifting is a serious problem from many standpoints. It is a social and economic problem, but, far more importantly, it is a spiritual problem. The Bible condemns stealing in no uncertain terms, and those who do so are going to be lost if they do not repent and turn in obedience to God's will.

To show you the relevance and reality of this matter, let me quote a few statistics. *U.S. News and World Report* (Nov. 28, 1977) says the following:

> Merchants this yuletide are bracing for a wave of shoplifting and employee theft that could easily exceed $1 billion dollars.

> About 500 million dollars will be lost to light-fingered shoppers and another 600 million to pilfering employees this year, according to Gordon Williams of the National Retail Merchants Association. The total will be swollen by another 400 million spent by merchants on loss prevention.

Time Magazine (Dec. 12, 1977), in an article entitled, "There Are 18 Shoplifting Days Till Christmas," also reports some interesting statistics:

> Shoppers who neglect to pay for their merchandise are criminals for all reasons, and their numbers are increasing at an alarming rate. The FBI reports more than 600,000 shoplifting arrests across the nation last year, nearly three times as many as in 1970, and the U.S. Department of Commerce estimates merchants' losses from thefts in 1976 at home $8 billion.

You may have noticed that these statistics I have quoted are not the most current. If the losses are estimated at $8 billion for 1976, think what they must be for this past year! Let me also

hasten to point out that the problem is not simply restricted to the poor or lower-class Americans. It is to be found in every class of our society.

Why Are So Many Involved in This Crime?

This is an interesting question and deserves our attention. I believe there are a number of reasons people decide to shoplift. Many steal due to psychological reasons I would be unqualified to deal with. I am afraid, however, that many are too quick to label everyone who engages in this criminal pastime as simply being "psychologically maladjusted." A lady wrote to Ann Landers once, complaining about her husband bringing things home from work that did not belong to him. Ann replied by saying that she should take him to a psychiatrist because he was "sick." They used to call such a one a thief. Certainly there are some who are psychologically maladjusted, and a psychiatrist probably could help; but let us not forget that most of those who engage in such actions are simply thieves and need to be identified as such.

But why are so many involved in this crime? Permit me to list a few of the most obvious reasons:

1. The tendency to rationalize. Those whom I have talked to about why they shoplifted generally say, "The prices are too high," "The stores are trying to rip us off so why not?" or "Everyone else is doing it." In other words, they are simply rationalizing their conduct. They are trying to convince themselves and others that there is nothing wrong with such conduct. Of course, no amount of rationalizing will make something right that is inherently wrong to begin with. Stealing in any way, shape, or form is wrong. It is sinful, and no amount of rationalizing will make it right. It was condemned in the Old Testament as well as in the New Testament. One of the Ten Commandments stated simply "Thou shalt not steal" (Exod. 20:15). Jesus endorsed this commandment in Matthew 19:18, as did the apostle Paul in Romans 13:9. Rationalizing will not remove or erase these verses from the Bible.

Such rationalizing begins early in life. Children will take money from mother's purse, thinking, "She doesn't need it" or "She has so much she won't miss this small amount." Sometimes children will take something from a parent as a means of retaliation because the parent disciplined the child or told the child "no." Sometimes parents will in a subtle way condone children's taking things that do not belong to them. This is often done because parents have guilty feelings about not giving their children as much time and attention as they should. Stealing seems to have a great deal to do with the issue

of entitlement—what a person feels is due him. Stealing or shoplifting, to such a one, is simply making up for something which is rightfully his, but which was denied him because of life's unfairness. These people say to themselves, "I have this coming to me."

Usually, the person who steals thinks that, at some point in the past, something that belonged to him was taken away. Thus, the person who steals sees himself as the victim rather than the perpetrator of a theft. Often he feels victory rather than guilt when he has successfully stolen some article from a store. Sometimes the motivation for

> Some people will shoplift simply for "kicks." They feel a sense of excitement from having "put one over" on their victim.

such action is based on the fact that the victim is impersonal rather than personal. They wouldn't think of robbing a man on the street, but if they take something from a big department store and get away with it, they feel they have simply "beaten the system." All this is rationalizing; it is convoluted thinking and in no way justifies the act of stealing.

2. Covetousness. This word is defined as "to wish for, especially eagerly; usually, to desire inordinately, or without due regard to the rights of others." There can be no doubt about it. This describes a shoplifter in every detail. He has an inordinate desire for something and has no consideration for the rights of anybody else.

The Bible also condemns such an attitude. Jesus warned the multitude in Luke 12:15, "Take heed, and beware of covetousness: for a man's life consisteth not in the abundance of the things which he possesseth." Paul described the condition of the Gentiles without the gospel in Romans 1:29: "Being filled with all unrighteousness, fornication, wickedness, covetousness, maliciousness." All one has to do is glance at a concordance to see the numerous warnings against the sin of covetousness. Shoplifting involves the sin of covetousness.

3. Sense of excitement. Some people will shoplift simply for "kicks." They feel a sense of excitement from having "put one over" on their victim. Those with this attitude enjoy the risk. They are very much like the gambler who also plays the odds for the sake of the big win and are quite willing to take the risk. Usually, they are aware of the security systems but feel they are far too smart or clever to be outdone by a store detective or a camera. Many feel that, if they are caught, they can get out of it by simply saying, "It was a mistake." Shoplifters are usually quite daring. I heard of one lady who boasted that she had shoplifted a garbage can. An article in the September 1977 issue of *Nation's Business* described an experiment that was conducted in one grocery store trying to find out if people would report a shoplifter if they saw one in action. The store detective walked up to the poultry department and stuffed a turkey under his coat and walked out the door. One person who witnessed the crime, deciding not to be outdone, stuffed one under his coat and also walked out. Daring indeed!

3. Desperation. The reason we might logically attribute one's becoming a shoplifter to is, in reality, very rare. Stealing or shoplifting has very little to do with poverty or the lack of basic necessities. So states Dr. James G. Blakemore, professor of Psychiatry, Vanderbilt University School of Medicine. This being the case, it becomes obvious that those who are saying that we can cure the ills of the world by giving everyone more education and more money simply do not have the answer.

What Is the Solution?

We have already quoted from the *U.S. News and World Report* article stating that $400 million was spent last year on loss prevention. Certainly this will help deter some from shoplifting, but this alone is not the answer. There is an interesting article in the December of 1978 issue of *Family Health* dealing with "mind manipulation." The stores under consideration use soft background music, but it is mixed with the voice of a person softly whispering, "Be honest, do not steal." The tape rolls on, "I am honest, I will not steal; if I do steal I will get caught and sent to jail." The message remains basically the same, being repeated some 9,000 times every hour. They say that prospective shoplifters walk out of the store scratching their heads, wondering why they did not take what they had intended. Is "mind manipulation" the answer?

Let me suggest another alternative. Let's take the gospel of Christ to men and women, boys and girls, and see if that will help. After all, it is the power of God unto salvation (Rom. 1:16). The Hebrew writer (4:12) said it is sharper than any two-edged-sword (and I might add that the gospel is sharper, than a mind-manipulating tape recorder). Paul said, "Let this mind be in you, which was also in Christ Jesus" (Phil. 2:5). Let's teach people the principles of righteousness contained in the word of God. Let's teach our young people that sin is real and that the consequences of sin are real; that whatsoever a man sows, that shall he also reap (Gal. 6:7). Let's teach people that truth is not something relative, but that God has an absolute standard of morality. It is reasonable, logical, ethical, and equitable. Let's teach people about the glories of heaven. Certainly that ought to motivate people to want to do right. Let's teach people what it means to be a Christian. The life of a Christian is satisfying, but not self-indulgent. What makes life great is to have something great to live for, and then to try to influence others to do the same. The Christian will learn to accept the authority

NOTES
_____
_____
_____
_____
_____
_____

of God and to be ruled by God's will, not self-will or man's will. This is the whole message of the Bible.

Shoplifting, like so many other subjects covered in this workbook, is simply a symptom. The real problem is basic disregard for right and wrong, and the word of God that shows us the distinction between the two.

Self-examination is difficult to practice. Rationalizing our conduct is extremely easy. Do not be deceived to think that stealing is extremely easy or can be condoned. We will be judged by God's word, and the word forbids such conduct. Parents, do not be deceived into thinking that your children would never do such a thing. Teach them that such is wrong, and why it is wrong.

Questions

Choose the Best Answer

_____ 1. While you are shopping, you see someone place an article of clothing under his coat. You should:
   A. Go up and ask him what he is doing.
   B. Ignore it, for it's not any of your business.
   C. Report what you have seen to one of the store clerks.

_____ 2. You have just walked out of a restaurant. As you look at your change, you realize the cashier gave you $5 too many. You should:
   A. Go back and return the money to the cashier.
   B. Keep the money. After all, there have been times when you were shortchanged.
   C. Put the money in the collection plate next Sunday.

_____ 3. You consider it a great honor to have been asked to join a fraternity at college. As one of the initiation rites, you and the other inductees are told you must shoplift an item from the local grocery store. You should:
   A. Buy the item and then tell the fraternity that you took it from the store.
   B. Make it known that you will not shoplift because it is condemned in the Bible.
   C. Go ahead and shoplift the item this one time.

_____ 4. After getting home from work, you discover you brought home one of the company's wrenches. You should:
   A. Keep it. After all they won't miss one little wrench.
   B. Return it.
   C. Throw it away.

True or False

_____ 1. The Bible says nothing about shoplifting.

_____ 2. Shoplifting is a social, economic, and a spiritual problem.

_____ 3. In 1976, merchants lost an estimated $3 billion due to shoplifting.

_____ 4. The reason people steal is that they are psychologically maladjusted.

_____ 5. There is nothing wrong with someone taking what he feels he has been cheated out of.

_____ 6. Covetousness can be a motive for shoplifting.

_____ 7. The best cure for shoplifting is for more stores to use mind manipulation tapes.

_____ 8. Ephesians 4:28 condemns stealing.

What's Wrong with These Excuses for Shoplifting?

1. "The stores are trying to rip us off, so why not?"_____

_____

_____

2. "Everyone else is doing it." _____

_____

_____

3. "They won't miss a small amount." _____

_____

_____

4. "I have it coming to me." _____

_____

_____

_____

_____

5. "It's fun to see if you can get away with it." _____

_____

_____

6. "I'm too poor to pay for the things I need." _____

_____

_____

Is Gambling Right? Don't Bet on It!

Larry Ray Hafley

Several years ago, the Institution for Social Research at the University of Michigan made an extensive study of gambling in the United States. The study revealed that, in 1974, two out of every three Americans made a bet. Gambling is a multibillion-dollar business of crime and sin. More than $30 billion is gambled each year in this country!

Definitions of Gambling

Gambling is defined by various sources as "to play games of chance for money or some other stake." "Gambling is the betting or staking of something of value, with consciousness of risk and hope of gain, on the outcome of a game, a contest, or an uncertain event whose result may be determined by chance or accident, or which may have an unexpected result by reason of the bettor's miscalculation."

What We Are Discussing

First, we are not discussing the stock market. One who "plays" the market purchases something of value. His money is used by the company. Both the buyer and the company may profit from the purchase of stock, or both may lose. The buyer may receive a return, a profit, or a loss in the business; this is economics, not gambling as we have defined it.

Second, we are not concerned with a farmer who takes a risk in planting his crops. He does not expect something for nothing. He does not profit at another's expense. His success benefits everyone and harms no one.

Third, we are not talking about the "gambling in the game of life." There is an element of risk in crossing a street, driving a car, and walking down a flight of stairs. This is not the issue.

Fourth, we are not arguing that the term "gamble" is in the Bible. It is not. One who wants to dispute that fact may have the field to himself. That is not the question before us.

Is Gambling Sinful?

"To gamble or not to gamble, that is the question" is the point of dispute. Gambling is sinful because:

1. It violates the principle of stewardship. The child of God is to be a faithful and wise steward (Luke 12:42; 1 Pet. 4:10; 1 Cor. 4:2). The prodigal son perhaps squandered part of his family fortune by gambling (Luke 15:13). Though it was his "portion of good," he had an obligation to use it wisely. The elder son recognized this when he sullenly said, "Thy son . . . hath devoured thy living with harlots." It was the younger boy's possession from the father. Our possessions come from our Father in heaven. Everything ultimately belongs to Him (Psa. 50:8-10), though there is a sense in which our possessions belong to us (Acts 5:4). As owners of our own possessions, we must oversee our share of this world's goods with the virtues of labor, benevolence, and thrift. Gambling is not a virtue. Would you want someone to take your gift and wager it?

2. It goes against the "golden rule" (Matt. 7:12). The Bible teaches that we are to love our neighbors as we do ourselves (Matt. 22:39), and "love worketh no ill to his neighbor" (Rom. 13:10). However, in gambling, if one is able to acquire his brother's goods by trickery or chance, it is simply "too bad." Can the gambler say he does unto others as he would they do unto him? No, the gambler's motto is, "I hope I can do it unto you *before* you do it unto me."

3. It is stealing. Murder is wrong, but, at times, men and nations have "legalized" duels (hence, murder by common consent). Likewise, men and nations have laws against stealing; yet, they often seek to legitimatize it and call it gambling. Do you think God approves of murder just because it was done under the strict rules of a duel? What makes you think he endorses thievery under the guise of gambling?

4. It contradicts the work ethic. The Bible teaches that men are to earn their bread by work, by the sweat of their brow (2 Thess. 3:10; Gen. 1:19). Granted, a gambler may have cause to sweat because of a large debt, but his "labor" is not productive. His winnings do not represent remuneration for the exchange of goods and services. Proverbs and Ecclesiastes extol the virtue of toil and of riches gained by honest labor. Gambling is not consistent with this view of work in the Scriptures; hence, it is sinful.

5. It exploits others. The Bible soundly condemns those who exploit others for their own advantage (Jas. 5:1-5). True, the text does not specifically deal with gambling, but the principle is the same. Observe a parallel. In James 2, the writer condemns partiality. The prejudicial treatment is based on wealth. James convicts respect of persons on the basis of wealth. The principle would apply in regard to racial discrimination. As we may use James 2:1-4 to condemn respect of persons based on race, though the text itself deals with wealth so we may use James 5:1-5 to condemn exploitation, though gambling is not the immediate subject.

6. It results in intemperance. The Lord requires moderation, temperance, or self-control in all things. Gambling is addictive. It maintains a grip on people like alcohol, cigarettes, drugs, and pornography do. To underscore that fact, there is a Gamblers Anonymous (GA) organization like the more famous Alcoholics Anonymous (AA). There are as many as 10 million compulsive gamblers in the United States! They are literally hooked on gambling. Perhaps not everything that is addictive is wrong, but gambling is an addiction which results in the loss of things that could be put to use in one's life in the world and in the service of God, and, as such, it is wrong.

7. It sets a bad example. Christians must be concerned about their influence for truth and righteousness (Matt. 5:13-16). Children of God must provide things honest in the sight of all men (Rom. 12:17; 2 Cor. 8:21). One must not give occasion for the devil to desecrate the word and name of God (1 Tim. 5:14; Tit. 2:5,10). Tertullian (AD 160-220) is reported to have said, "If you say you are a Christian when you are a dice player, you say what you are not, because you are a partner with the world."

8. It breeds other sins. In Reno, Nevada, the police department estimates that 75 percent of their embezzlement cases are related to gambling. Gambling corrupts and corrodes character. Dishonesty and deceit are its fruits, and a tree is known by its fruits (Matt. 7:16-18). As drug addicts resort to stealing and prostitution to support their habit, so do gamblers use vice to sustain their habit. When it is observed that 75 percent of all murders involve the use of alcohol, people are often quick to condemn drinking. If 75 percent of embezzlement cases involve gambling in Reno, should one let gambling stand without opposition?

9. It destroys the home. Nearly every gospel preacher or marriage counselor has seen the adverse effects of gambling on a marriage or home. One beset by alcohol adversely affects others and destroys his family, and so does the gambler. In Reno, Nevada, for example, there is an organization called Gam Anon for families that are torn asunder by gambling. Surely, anything that besmirches the sanctity of the home is wrong.

10. It puts one with evil companions. It is a generally accepted fact that organized crime profits from most public gambling. Gambling attracts evil men like a dead animal lures a vulture. Gamblers are not known as spiritually-minded people. Gamblers are identified with drinking and immorality of all kinds. "Evil companionships corrupt good manners" (1 Cor. 15:33), and Paul said, "Have no fellowship with the unfruitful works of darkness, but rather reprove them" (Eph. 5:11).

You Categorize Gambling

Let us now put the ball in your court. Paul said that we are to "deny (1) ungodliness and (2) worldly lusts," and that "we should live (1) soberly, (2) righteously, and (3) godly in this present world" (Titus 2:11-12). In which category would you place gambling? Would you think it strange if you should see a Christian whom you greatly admire engaged in gambling? You be the judge.

What about "Innocent" Bets?

The question always arises. "I know it's wrong to gamble, but at the office we match pennies to see who buys the coffee" or "We have a little 'pool' for every heavyweight title fight and the World Series. Nobody puts in more than a dollar. It's harmless. Is that wrong?" Gamblers Anonymous, the organization designed to help compulsive gamblers, urges its members not to gamble on who buys the coffee. They see a danger. The bitter fruits of gambling do not make permissible even a little bet. Do not take a chance that a little gambling will not hurt. A defense of "innocent, little bets" is like condemning alcoholism but then having someone attempt to justify "just one beer after work." Christians should shun the very appearance of evil (Prov. 1:10; 1 Thess. 5:21). This means do not bet on gambling, not even a little. You will be the loser both here and hereafter.

Questions

Which Column?

(Place the items below in the correct column on the chart.)

Gambling	Non-Gambling

1. Matching pennies

2. Purchasing stocks

3. Buying lottery tickets

4. Entering sporting pools

5. Buying insurance

Matching (Match the Scripture with its teaching.)

_____ 1. A steward should be faithful.   A. Matthew 7:17

_____ 2. Everything is God's.   B. James 5:4

_____ 3. We should treat others as we want to be treated.   C. 1 Corinthians 4:2

_____ 4. We should love our neighbor as ourselves.   D. Matthew 7:12

_____ 5. We should work, or not eat.   E. 1 Corinthians 15:33

_____ 6. Fraud is condemned.   F. Romans 12:17

_____ 7. We should provide things honest in the sight   G. 2 Thessalonians 3:10

   of all men.   H. Psalm 50:10

_____ 8. A corrupt tree brings forth evil fruit.   I. Matthew 22:39

_____ 9. Evil companions corrupt good morals.

Do You Agree or Disagree?

1. "Gambling is simply taking a risk." _____

2. "Gambling is not mentioned in the Bible, so it cannot be wrong." _____

3. "According to Acts 5:4, we can use our money as we please." _____

4. "Gambling is just another form of stealing." _____

5. "Gambling can become an addictive habit." _____

6. "Gambling can lead to other sins." _____

7. "It doesn't hurt to make little bets occasionally." _____

8. "If the government legalizes gambling, like buying lottery tickets, then such is no longer wrong."

   _____

   _____

Lesson 19

Profanity

David Dann

As Christians, we are commanded to "seek those things which are above, where Christ is, sitting at the right hand of God" (Col. 3:1). The child of God is expected to live in such a way so that his primary focus is upon serving and pleasing the Lord (Matt. 6:33). Those who fail in this regard have often failed due to the fact that they have succumbed to profanity.

What Is Profanity?

1. The definition of "profane." The word "profane" in our English New Testaments is translated from the word *bebelos*, which is defined as "permitted to be trodden, accessible" (Vine, 490). A.T. Robertson adds that the word refers to that which is "trodden under foot, unhallowed" (Vol. V: 438). It is evident that "profane" carries such a connotation in modern English. Webster defines it as "showing contempt of sacred things, irreverent."

2. References to "profane" in the Old Testament. This word often appears in Old Testament passages with reference to the irreverent attitudes, words, and actions displayed by Israel. The Scriptures speak of how they profaned the name of God (Lev. 18:21; Jer. 34:16), the Sabbath (Ezek. 20:16), and the holy things of the sanctuary (Ezek. 22:26). Profanity was displayed when God's people turned their back on Him, disrespected His laws, and treated that which was holy as though it were common.

3. References to "profane" in the New Testament. The word occurs in the following five passages in the New Testament:

> Knowing this: that the law is not made for a righteous person, but for the lawless and insubordinate, for the ungodly and for sinners, for the unholy and profane, for murderers of fathers and murderers of mothers, for manslayers . . . (1 Tim. 1:9).

> But reject profane and old wives' fables, and exercise yourself toward godliness (1 Tim. 4:7).

> O Timothy! Guard what was committed to your trust, avoiding the profane and idle babblings and contradictions of what is falsely called knowledge (1 Tim. 6:20).

> But shun profane and idle babblings, for they will increase to more ungodliness (2 Tim. 2:16).

> Lest there be any fornicator or profane person like Esau, who for one morsel of food sold his birthright (Heb. 12:16).

It is significant that the Hebrew writer illustrates the profane mindset by making reference to Esau. He is put forward as one who demonstrates profanity because he treated something sacred (his birthright) with contempt and irreverence by selling it in order to satisfy a common desire—hunger. The New Testament uses of the word to show that "profane" is closely connected with that which is unholy and those who are uninterested in holy things.

Profanity in Religion

While profanity is often thought of as wholly separate from and unconnected with religion, remember that the Israelites committed profanity within the context of practicing religion (Ezek. 22:26). We must not ignore the reality of profanity in religion. There are a number of ways in which those who profess to be Christians display profanity in religion.

1. Tolerating sin in the church. The church is the body of Christ (Col. 1:18). As such, we are cautioned against defiling it in any way (1 Cor. 3:16-17). The church is profaned when sin and immorality are tolerated among the members of the local congregation. Profanity among the denominations has come to be expected in many cases where those engaged in immoral behavior, such as homosexuals, are tolerated and welcomed into fellowship, in spite of the clear teaching of Scripture (1 Cor. 6:9-11; 5:11-13). Let us not think that this sort of profanity is limited to the denominational realm. Where adulterous marriages, social drinking, immodest and lascivious dress, and other sins are tolerated, the local church has been profaned.

2. Secularizing the church. The mission and purpose of the church are suited to meet the spiritual needs of man, rather than his worldly and physical needs (1 Tim. 3:15). When the church becomes involved in serving the social and recreational needs of the community, it has been profaned (Rom. 14:17). Additionally, the way of God is profaned by those who change the spiritual mission of the church into a mission focused on feeding and clothing the world and righting the social ills of the day. The church is profaned when it is made into a secular institution.

3. Ignoring God's instruction. God has given us a perfect guide in religion in the Scriptures (2 Tim. 3:16-17). Where God's word is trampled on in favor of human wisdom, there is profanity in religion. This profanity is seen in the use of mechanical instruments of music in worship (Eph. 5:19), the use of women in leadership positions over men (1 Tim. 2:11-12), and any other substitution or innovation that is enacted without regard for the word of God. When the New Testament pattern for the work, worship, and organization of the church is cast aside profanity is in full bloom.

Profanity in Everyday Life

We probably most often think of profanity outside of the context of religion. It is usually referenced in connection with a person's speech and conduct. The Christian must be on guard against the profanity that is prevalent in our society and culture.

> **Profane speech reveals a profane heart.**

1. We are constantly confronted with profanity. The Bible associates profanity with anything that is against sound doctrine (1 Tim. 1:9). Who can dispute the amount of unholy, immoral, and irreverent behavior that is depicted in movies, on television, in music, and on the Internet? The faithful Christian should be offended by and turn away from the profanity that has engulfed our media and our culture (Rom. 12:1-2). But do we turn away from it? What are we filling our minds with? The one who says that the foul language he hears in the movies will not affect him has already been affected more than he thinks!

2. Profane speech. The profane person thinks nothing of making irreverent references to God and Christ in his everyday conversation. But the profanity doesn't end there. It is popular to tell dirty jokes. You may not be the one telling them, but too many are finding enjoyment in listening to them. Others cannot seem to complete a sentence without including some sort of curse or swear word. Some feel justified because they only use those foul words when they are really upset or angry. For the Christian, there is no justification for profanity in speech. We are told, "But now you yourselves are to put off all these: anger, wrath, malice, blasphemy, filthy language out of your mouth" (Col. 3:8). Paul also says, "Let no corrupt word proceed out of your mouth, but what is good for necessary edification, that it may impart grace to the hearers" (Eph. 4:29). Many have sought to soften the offensive nature of their speech by using "euphemisms" such as "golly," "gee," "gosh," "darn," and "heck" rather than use the words that are considered really bad. This may seem to make their language less offensive, but it is no less profane. It is especially disheartening to hear Christians using these words. Profane speech reveals a profane heart (Matt. 12:34). Guard your tongue. Stop and think before you utter something profane. "For by your words you will be justified, and by your words you will be condemned" (Matt. 12:37).

3. **Profane actions.** Profanity is certainly seen in the lives of those who are too busy seeking after pleasure to acknowledge their Creator. They are too self-absorbed to have any reverence or regard for the God who made them. The Bible says that such people as these, "are without excuse" (Rom. 1:20-21). However, one need not be an atheist in order to exhibit a profane lifestyle. Many Christians live profane lives simply by placing worldly matters ahead

of serving the Lord. Profanity is prevalent when parents make time for their children to be involved in Little League and Scouts, but cannot find time to bring them to Bible study, gospel meetings, or teach them God's word at home. Profane parents help their children become star athletes and honor students but do very little to "bring them up in the training and admonition of the Lord" (Eph. 6:4). As a result, they raise profane children who grow up to be profane adults. They may attend with the church as long as their parents make them, but as soon as they are old enough to make their own decisions, they will be off pursuing the worldly goals that their profane parents taught them to place ahead of spiritual things. Don't be surprised if this scenario sounds familiar. Profanity is popular.

Questions

Matching

_____ 1. Profane

_____ 2. Eupemisms

_____ 3. Perfect guide in religion

_____ 4. The mouth speaks

_____ 5. Profane person

_____ 6. Profane and idle babblings

A. Esau

B. Out of the abundance of the heart

C. Permitted to be trodden

D. Increase to more ungodliness

E. Mild word used in place of an offensive one

F. The Scriptures

True of False:

_____ 1. The only people who live a profane lifestyle are those who are not religious.

_____ 2. One can profane the church by changing the pattern of worship given in the New Testament.

NOTES

_____
_____
_____
_____
_____
_____

_____ 3.   It is okay to listen to dirty jokes as long as you are not the one telling them.

_____ 4.   We have no control over the foul language we hear on television and in the movies.

_____ 5.   Some children quit worshiping God because their parents failed to raise them properly.

_____ 6.   Profanity only has reference to our speech.

Discussion

1.   The Israelites committed profanity in religion. Describe how the church can be profaned today in the following areas:

   a.   Morality: _____
   _____
   _____

   b.   The worship of the church: _____
   _____
   _____

   c.   The mission of the church: _____
   _____
   _____

2.   Why is Esau considered a profane person (Heb. 12:16)? _____
   _____
   _____

3.   How can we guard against the profanity that may come from the following sources?

   a.   Television: _____
   _____
   _____

   b.   Movies: _____
   _____
   _____

   c.   Music: _____
   _____
   _____

   d.   Friends and coworkers: _____
   _____
   _____

4.   Is it wrong to use euphemisms? Why or why not? _____
   _____
   _____

Respectable Worldliness

Hiram Hutto

To trace the development of the word *kosmos*, from which "world" is translated, is an interesting, if somewhat disappointing exercise. Initially the word meant an ornament, then the ordered or beautiful arrangement of the universe, next the earth, then the inhabitants of the earth—most of whom are bad—and thus finally the evil that characterizes the world. The word "worldliness" started out meaning something beautiful and attractive, but ended up meaning something bad and ugly. Most sin is that way. It can take something good and lovely and misuse it so that the result is evil. And this is doubly demonstrated in the title of this article. Doubly, because it takes something good and misuses it; but then to compound the tragedy, the bad is endorsed and becomes respectable so that something evil is portrayed as something good! "Woe unto them that call evil good, and good evil" (Isa. 5:20). But perhaps you wonder: Just what is *"respectable worldliness"*?

Let it be noted to begin with that by respectable worldliness I do not mean that such is respectable with God. The very concept behind worldliness eliminates any idea of God's approval of it. John tells us that it "is not of the Father" (1 John 2:16), and James says, "Friendship with the world is enmity with God" (Jas. 4:4).

Just as goodness stems from the good, and kindness from the kind, so worldliness stems from the world ("the lust of the flesh, and the lust of the eyes, and the pride of life"—1 John 2:16). It has both its origin and fruition in the kind of thinking and/or action which springs from such considerations. Fundamentally, worldliness is an emphasis (which often runs to obsession) on that which is temporal, material, and physical (which frequently involves the sensual), rather than that which is spiritual. It is the opposite of spirituality. Clearly this can involve "a multitude of sins" (Jas. 5:20). As a rule, however, worldliness is thought of in terms of that which is either immoral or tends to immorality, and, to be sure, there are

> There are many others to whom immorality is abhorrent, who nonetheless have little or no interest in God or spiritual things; who emphasize the material, the physical at the expense of, and all too frequently, to the exclusion of, the spiritual. All such are worldly.

many worldly people who hate both God and all who would live godly lives. Yet there are many others to whom immorality is abhorrent, who nonetheless have little or no interest in God or spiritual things and who emphasize the material (the physical) at the expense of, and, all too frequently, to the exclusion of, the spiritual. All such are worldly. They "mind earthly things" (Phil. 3:19). And they not only do this in their own lives, but so uphold it, exalt it, and encourage it, that such have come to be looked upon by most people as not only not degrading, but positively desirable, and respectable.

By respectable worldliness, then, I do not mean the immoral, the vulgar, the sensual, but rather that which the world considers respectable, and this in areas that in themselves are honorable, noble, and upright. This has had its influence on the church. For example, I do not preach to many people who are murderers or bank robbers. I would like to think that most assemblies to whom I preach are not characterized by too many adulterers (and one would be too many to be a part of the people of God) or drunkards. And chances are good that most in these audiences would find such repugnant. Yet they have been so affected by the world's standard of respectability that many are guilty of respectable worldliness, and without some intense vigilance, many more will be. Let me illustrate.

An industrious brother (concerned about the high cost of living, the needs of his family, and the requisites of a good education for them) takes a second job. This he does, knowing when he does it that it will entail his being unable to assemble with the saints as the word of God teaches, and if not that, surely knowing that it will preclude his being available for any significant amount of his individual responsibilities in the church.

As the world looks on this type of individual, he has many respectable qualities. He is concerned about his family's financial welfare and future. He is no leech on society. He wants to provide for his own, and even the Bible endorses this (1 Tim. 5:8). *But he attains a lesser goal at the expense of a more important one.* The one he attains may be good, noble, and respectable, but it is "worldly" nevertheless, because it emphasizes the physical and material at the expense of the spiritual. And certainly he has not sought "first the kingdom of God and his righteousness" (Matt. 6:33).

And what shall I say about working mothers? First of all, I want to say, because the Bible shows that *they do have a right to work!* But the word of God also tells them where to work. It does not say "good secretaries, excellent clerks, workers in factories." It says "workers at *home*, keepers at *home*" (Titus 2:5). 1 Timothy 5:14 shows that there is more to this than sweeping floors and washing the dishes. It says "guide the home." This is a spiritual endeavor, and to "farm it out" so as to increase income for *things* is to exchange the spiritual for the material. How depressing that people no longer believe that the hand that rocks the cradle is the hand that rules the world. What a tragedy that Christian mothers have allowed themselves to be cheated out of one of the noblest of tasks by having the false idea foisted upon them that they cannot

> How depressing that people no longer believe that the hand that rocks the cradle is the hand that rules the world. What a tragedy that Christian mothers have allowed themselves to be cheated out of one of the noblest of tasks by having the false idea foisted upon them that they cannot be "fulfilled" unless they get out of the house and into the business world.

be "fulfilled" unless they get out of the house and into the business world. So successfully (respectably) has this been done that *16 million* American mothers with children under age 18 work outside the home. Forty percent (40%) of the women who have children under six years of age leave them with somebody else while they go off to work. What is it that prompts such? Will it help these Christian women participate more in "church work"? Will it increase their opportunities to visit the sick, to attend Bible classes, and do many other activities in the Lord's work? I do not recall ever hearing anyone say, "I think leaving my children to someone else will help them and me grow spiritually." Quite a few just "took the job temporarily, till we get these unusual expenses paid." (And these often turn out to be about as temporary as taxes!) I visit in some of these homes, and from what I observe, they certainly could not be said to be in any kind of dire financial circumstances. Most of them are in financial circumstances as good as most and better than many. Was it spiritual reasons that demanded they so do? And consider this:

1. The training of children is not the responsibility of the government. It is not the responsibility of the grandparents, and not the responsibility of baby-sitters. It is the responsibility of fathers (Eph. 6:4) and mothers (1 Tim. 5:14). It is a spiritual activity and no part-time job.

2. Who is going to be the source of "influence" on that child while his mother is away at work? Who will nurse him when he cries, kiss his bruised knees, warn him against the dangers that lie ahead? Does the day-care center really care about the kind of TV being watched?

3. Frequently such arrangements allow the child to spend most of his waking hours with someone other than his mother. I have even

known children who called their sitters—rather than their own mothers—by the name "Mother."

4. It is an open secret that many, many wives are too tired after a "hard day at the office" to be the spiritual influence and companion that they need to be.

5. We will not discuss the resentment, temptations, etc. that come her way. But for two excellent lessons dealing with this entire subject, see one by Horace Huggins and another by James Cope in the 1979 Florida College Lecture book.

If having mothers working outside the home results in emphasis on the material at the expense of the spiritual (and the evidence seems overwhelming), it is worldliness. The fact that the world may "respect" it does not change the world nature of this scenario.

Free Time

Vacations exert a wholesome influence. They can refresh the individual and stimulate a renewed vigor in the return to normal activity, and I believe such can be justified by the Scriptures. But Christians can never take a vacation from God! This is true whether it involves a two-week vacation or simply a weekend at the lake. But there are many members of the church who abuse such blessings and, during these times, emphasize the material and physical at the ex-pense of the spiritual, and that's worldliness. The spiritually-minded person does nothing before considering it in the light of how it will fit in with the will of God for his life. Of primary importance is the question of whether the proposed activity will this allow me to discharge my obligation and enjoy the privileges of being a child of God?

1. **What shall I do?** There are many things that the world calls respectable that a child of God cannot engage in because he has a different standard. Since other articles in this workbook have discussed such questionable activities, I forego a discussion of them here.

2. **Where shall I go?** Those who are concerned about this world will consider the scenery, and the entertainment (and there is plenty of this that is respectable), but the spiritually-minded person, while he can enjoy the scenery and the respectable entertainment,

is primarily concerned with such things as whether there will be an opportunity to worship with God's people while away from home. Far too many members of the church wait till Saturday or Sunday morning, if then, to "look for a Church of Christ." The spiritually-minded did that before he left home. I am thrilled that I know a teenager who toured the western states with a foreign friend, but before beginning, wrote various congregations along the route to insure attendance at church services would be possible. And I cannot emphasize it too strongly: A Christian ought to have the same convictions away from home that he has at home! If he cannot conscientiously worship with a liberal congregation at home, he ought not to worship with one away from home. Just having up a sign that says "church of Christ" is not enough. A Christian wants the vacation, but not at the expense of spiritual considerations.

There are members who get very involved in civic affairs, all of which may be perfectly good and wholesome (respectable). However, they can become so involved in them, that some even miss church services to attend to such. And I am delighted that I know others who let it be known to begin with that, with them, God comes first, and they will engage in nothing at any time that interferes.

> When a person takes only the materialistic and physical into consideration in choosing a wife or husband, he is making a grave mistake.

Marriage

Perhaps the problem that eventually led to the flood was begun when the children of God began to be more concerned with the physical beauty ("fair") than they were with spiritual qualities (Gen. 6:1-2). When a person takes only the materialistic and physical into consideration in choosing a wife or husband, he is making a grave mistake. These may be respectable considerations, but they are too often at the expense of the spiritual. Is she attractive? Does he have a well-paying job? (And this does not mean that you must try to find the ugliest one around, nor one who is "on welfare." Ugliness is no guarantee of spirituality, and laziness is certainly no virtue.) The thing that really matters is the spiritual. Is he a faithful Christian? (Do not merely ask, "Is he a member of the church?") Will she help me in the rearing of our children to be Christians? What are his spiritual qualities? Is he actively engaged in the Lord's work? Companions may be respectable in the eyes of the world by the world's standards (she is beautiful; he is successful), but what about in the eyes of God?

These are but a few of the many areas that demonstrate the need to be concerned about "respectable worldliness." Those involved in it usually bear very little, if any, fruit for God, but, like those sown on the thorny ground, "the cares of this world, and the deceitfulness of riches, and the lusts of other things entering in, choke the word, and . . . become unfruitful" (Mark 4:19).

Attitudes That Prompt Worldliness

1. An erroneous evaluation of life. This attitude says things like "here and now." In so doing it turns the world upside down. It puts the world on top and the kingdom somewhere below that. It says, "I will seek the physical and the material, and then I will add the kingdom of God later."

a. **Things Come First.** Yet, Jesus said, "A man's life does not consist in the abundance of the things which he possesses" (Luke 12:15). Respectable worldliness contradicts this.

b. **Time.** This attitude says, "Later." The Bible says, "Boast not thyself of tomorrow; for thou knowest not what a day may bring forth" (Prov. 27:1). Respectable worldliness fails to properly evaluate life.

2. Satisfaction With Mere Membership. No need is felt to supply something for the edifying of the body (Eph. 4:16).

3. Indifferent to Individual Growth and Development. The admonition of Peter to "grow in grace and knowledge of our Lord and Savior Jesus Christ" (2 Pet. 3:18) is not appreciated. All such will remain spiritual dwarfs or babies.

4. A "Freeloader" and a Sponge. They have a "let-George-do-it" attitude.

5. Nearsighted. ". . . Seeing only the things that are near" in this world, such are mindful of this world, rather than seeking the one that is to come (see Heb. 11:14-15 for the proper evaluation).

What Is the Remedy for Respectable Worldliness?

1. Recognize the danger. In fact, in some ways it is even more dangerous than the immoral and the ungodly. This will indeed sap the very vitality from a person's spiritual well-being, but it does not look all that bad. One of its most fearful dangers is in its subtlety. This type of worldliness stems from what appears to be respectable motives: so many others are engaged in it, etc.

2. Look at things through the eyes of God. Before beginning any activity, ask yourself, "What will this do with my relationship with God? Would I want to appear before God right now? Will it allow, yea, even encourage, my wholehearted participation in all phases of His work, both in the church and as an individual Christian?"

3. Seek transformation, rather than conformation. Never be content to be as the world is or as it approves. Remember that "God does not see as man seeth" (1 Sam. 16:7), and His ways are higher than man's ways (Isa. 55:8-9). "And be not conformed to this world, but be ye transformed by the renewing of your mind" (Rom. 12:2).

4. Get involved in the work of the church.

5. Seek the association of other Christians. Perhaps it would be better to seek the association of those who are somewhat ahead of us in spiritual development. If you want to be a better tennis player, play with someone a little better than you are. If you want to develop spiritually, be with those who are a little more spiritually advanced than you are.

Consequences of Respectable Worldliness

1. God is robbed. If there is ever a time when we do not give God that which is rightfully His, we are robbing God. Since we are to "seek ye first his kingdom and his righteousness" (Matt. 6:33), to put anything else first (and that is exactly what respectable worldliness does) is to rob him of what belongs to Him.

2. The church is robbed. If you do not share in the work and function of the congregation, it is being deprived of your talent and time.

3. The individual is robbed. He is robbed of spiritual development. He is robbed of true peace of mind. He is robbed of the contribution of that most valuable possession, himself. And worst of all, he may be robbed of his soul in heaven for "the world passeth away and the lusts thereof, but he that doeth the will of God abideth forever" (1 John 2:17).

NOTES
_____
_____
_____
_____
_____
_____

Questions

Multiple Choice

_____ 1. The Greek word for worldliness is (a. *kardia*, b. *kosmos*, c. *bapto*).

_____ 2. Worldliness eliminates (a. God, b. our family, c. ourselves).

_____ 3. Worldliness emphasizes (a. the beautiful, b. the physical, c. the spiritual).

_____ 4. The kind of worldliness which seems to affect the Christian the most is (a. immoral worldliness, b. vulgar worldliness, c. respectable worldliness).

_____ 5. Mothers should be workers (a. in a factory, b. in an office, c. at home).

_____ 6. (a. Forty percent, b. Forty-five percent, c. Fifty percent) of the women who have children under six years of age leave them with somebody else while they go off to work.

_____ 7. The training of children is the work of (a. the government, b. the parents, c. the church).

_____ 8. The most important thing in choosing a mate is (a. looks, b. family background, c. spiritual character).

_____ 9. Respectable worldliness can cause me to lose (a. my soul, b. my family, c. my friends).

Yes or No

_____ 1. Does sin always start out bad and ugly?

_____ 2. Can one be engaged in things that are right within themselves and yet still be guilty of worldliness?

_____ 3. Can mothers do work outside the home and not neglect their family duties?

_____ 4. Does the practice of members going out of town frequently on the weekends hinder the local church of which they are members?

_____ 5. Does it matter what kind of church we worship with when we are on vacation?

_____ 6. Can a Christian marry a non-Christian and have great hopes of converting him after their marriage?

_____ 7. Can a Christian imitate the world?

_____ 8. Should a Christian be spiritually farsighted?

Matching (Match the verse with its teaching.)

_____ 1. We should not call evil good.

_____ 2. Friendship with the world is enmity with God.

_____ 3. The lust of the flesh, the lust of the eye, and the pride of the life are of the world.

_____ 4. Life does not consist in the abundance of things.

_____ 5. We should not conform to the world.

_____ 6. God's kingdom should always come first.

_____ 7. One who does the will of God abides forever.

A. Romans 12:2

B. James 4:4

C. Luke 12:15

D. 1 John 2:17

E. 1 John 2:16

F. Isaiah 5:20

G. Matthew 6:33

Gospel Preachers Cannot Compromise on Worldliness

Mike Willis

When I was young enough to barely remember going to worship services, I distinctly recall attending a gospel meeting at a congregation located not far from my home at which the preacher condemned worldliness. He preached extensively about the sin of worldliness and condemned the very appearance of evil. Finally, he came to the application of his lesson and applied the passages pertaining to worldliness to playing dominoes. About ten to fifteen people responded to the invitation that night, primarily to confess unfaithfulness in the matter of worldliness. I specifically remember the young, local preacher personally confessing his worldliness in playing dominoes.

Things have indeed changed since those days. When I was a lad, the brethren discussed whether playing cards and dominoes were sinful in an effort to avoid any resemblance of interest in things worldly or doubtful. Even when some practices which did not violate a clear Bible principle were condemned (as in the case above), *an earnest effort was made to oppose worldliness and to keep the church pure!* Today the "clergy" is discussing whether or not homosexuality, prostitution, fornication, gambling, and any number of other sins are wrong, and churches are filled with such filth. In fact, many of the things condemned in the Bible as being sinful have now been legalized and become respectable in American culture. In many cases, *no effort* is made to oppose worldliness and to keep the church pure. I am reminded of Paul's statement, "for the fashion (*schema*) of this world passeth away" (i.e., it is constantly in a state of flux and change; 1 Cor. 7:31).

I must frankly confess that I liked the old days better, when the distinction between right and wrong was clearly admitted and acknowledged. Those were the days in which the majority of sinners practiced undercover sins because society as a whole rejected them because of their immorality. Yet, I cannot find a time machine which enables me to be removed from this

decade and placed in that of a few years ago. All things considered, I am not even sure that I would want to be. Yet, I do admit that I liked the moral conduct of the old society better than that which exists today.

> I believe that there are literally thousands of Americans who are sick and tired of clergymen pussyfooting with Satan and who would like to hear what the everlasting gospel has to say about morality.

Gospel Preachers and Worldliness

I have been disappointed in the stand which so-called "preachers" have taken on any number of issues relating to morality. I have seen denominational clergymen on television defending homosexuality and stating that the Bible teaches that we should love everyone and not condemn others simply because they have a different form of sexual expression from that which we have. I have heard radio programs in which preachers discussed the topic, "When is lying not lying?" I have participated in a talk radio program in which a denominational preacher refused to "condemn" prostitutes for their sin in his special ministry to prostitutes. Indeed, the denominational world around us has capitulated on the subject of morality.

It appears to me that this period of time should be especially ripe for preaching what the Bible says about morality. I believe that there are literally thousands of Americans who are sick and tired of clergymen pussyfooting with Satan and who would like to hear what the everlasting gospel has to say about morality. I think that they are tired of hearing discourses on nuclear power plants, guerrillas in South America, communal living, and other such social topics. I think that they would appreciate good gospel preaching on such topics as clean, godly living.

Unfortunately, the likelihood of their hearing these kinds of sermons is diminishing. Not a few of those who purport to be gospel preachers are compromising on the subject of worldliness. In an age that is being threatened by the evils of overindulgence in alcoholic beverages, some gospel preachers are defending social drinking. In an age that is crazed by sexual stimulation through immodest apparel, some gospel preachers are participating in mixed bathing. In an age when divorce and remarriage for unscriptural reasons are becoming socially accepted, and the American family is being unscripturally altered, some gospel preachers are teaching that those guilty of destroying homes through fornication have the scriptural right to remarry. Uncertain sounds are coming from the trumpets of those who should be sounding clarion notes for repentance.

Some of the stories which I hear regarding gospel preachers scare me inasmuch as they indicate what is no longer being preached. I have talked with men who relate that they had a discussion with another preacher regarding whether or not social drinking was wrong. I have been told of preachers who were housed in motels during gospel meetings being found engaging in mixed swimming when the local evangelist stopped by. On some occasions, the local evangelist simply jumped in the pool with them. Others among us are heavy smokers. These things indicate at least this to me: these men are not preaching against social drinking, mixed bathing, and smoking!

I am saddened to hear of a preaching brother becoming involved in some gross act of immorality, such as fornication. Usually, however, such a man humbly repents before God, tries to reconstruct his life on the basis of God's word, and resolves to serve the Lord throughout the remainder of his life. I have compassion for such a brother and suffer with him through the agonies which his sin brings to him. However, I know that this man will continue to preach against worldliness, perhaps even holding himself up as an example of how it can cause any of us to fall.

Such does not happen among those involved in social drinking and mixed bathing. Most of them are unwilling to admit that what they are doing is sinful. They are persuaded that there is nothing wrong with it, except that some old-fashioned brethren think that it is wrong. Hence, they must practice their sins in an undercover manner, lest these "old fogeys" detect them. Having reached these conclusions, such brethren will not repent of the immorality which they are practicing. Rather, they will continue to practice these sinful acts in secret.

This erosion of moral conviction among preachers is sometimes seen in secret lasciviousness, followed by secret fornication, followed by a cover-up. They refuse to repent, they run from their error by moving to a new area, and they either explicitly lie when questioned or else implicitly lie by maintaining a "righteous" silence. Those who refuse to repent of worldliness and who "get away with it" are likely to repeat and increase their sins.

How long has it been since you heard a good sermon on such things as dancing, mixed bathing, social drinking, and other forms of worldliness? Are we no longer hearing these kinds of sermons because these sins no longer pose a threat to the spiritual development of Christians? Have they quit being practiced by the society around us and no longer are in vogue? We all know the answers to these questions! The reason that some brethren are no longer preaching on these subjects is that they have become convinced that they are not sinful!

The Unchangeable Word

Yet, my brethren, God's word has not changed in this generation. It is the same today as it was in the first century. What it teaches about worldliness is still true, regardless of who teaches otherwise. Read its condemnation of ungodly behavior.

Now the works of the flesh are manifest, which are these: adultery, fornication, uncleanness, lasciviousness, idolatry, witchcraft, hatred, variance, emulations, wrath, strife, seditions, heresies, envyings, murders, drunkenness, revellings and such like: of the which I tell you before, as I have also told you in time past, that they which do such things shall not inherit the kingdom of God (Gal. 5:19-21).

Mortify therefore your members which are upon the earth; fornication, uncleanness, inordinate, affection, evil concupiscence, and covetousness, which is idolatry: for which things' sake the wrath of God cometh on the children of disobedience: in the which ye also walked some time, when ye lived in them. But now ye also put off all these; anger, wrath, malice, blasphemy, filthy communication out of your mouth. Lie not one to another, seeing that ye have put off the old man with his deeds; and have put on the new man, which is renewed in knowledge after the image of him that created him (Col. 3:5-10).

And even as they did not like to retain God in their knowledge, God gave them over to a reprobate mind, to do those things which are not convenient; being filled with all unrighteousness, fornication, wickedness, covetousness, maliciousness; full of envy, murder, debate, deceit, malignity; whisperers, backbiters, haters of God, despiteful, proud, boasters, inventors of evil things, disobedient to parents, without understanding covenant breakers, without natural affection, implacable, unmerciful; who knowing the judgment of God, that they which commit such things are worthy of death, not only do the same, but have pleasure in them that do them (Rom. 1:28-32).

The Scriptures speak just as certainly today regarding the condemnation of these acts of wickedness as they ever did at any time in the past. Though time has changed, societies have changed their laws, denominational preachers have changed their beliefs, and American culture has treated as respectable things which God has condemned, God's word remains the same.

In a time when denom AD inational clergymen and, unfortunately, some "gospel preachers" (I use the term accommodatively; when these men quit preaching what the gospel has to say about these subjects, they ceased to be worthy of the description "gospel preacher") have quit preaching on such topics as worldliness, and some among them have actually begun to defend what the Bible specifically condemns as sinful, we need to pay special attention to Paul's warning, "Be not deceived!" He wrote:

> Know ye not that the unrighteous shall not inherit the kingdom of God? Be not deceived. neither fornicators, nor idolaters, nor adulterers, nor effeminate, nor abusers of themselves with mankind, nor thieves, nor covetous, nor drunkards, nor revilers, nor extortioners, shall inherit the kingdom of God (1 Cor. 6:9-10).

Let us be careful that we are not deceived on these matters. What God has said shall not be changed by the presumptuous words of twentieth-century clergymen!

> Radio and television hosts, news commentators, justices, and practically everyone else have defended homosexuals; similarly, they have hurled every kind of disparaging remark imaginable at those who have done what they could to condemn homosexuality as sinful.

A Corrupted Society

Ours is indeed a corrupted society. It reminds me of that society which existed during the days of Isaiah. He mentioned a group of men who had blurred the distinction between right and wrong. Condemningly he wrote, "Woe unto them that call evil good, and good evil; that put darkness for light, and light for darkness; that put bitter for sweet, and sweet for bitter" (Isa. 5:20). If you think that this has not happened in America, look around you. Witness what has happened with reference to homosexuality. Radio and television hosts, news commentators, justices, and practically everyone else have defended homosexuals; similarly, they have hurled every kind of disparaging remark imaginable at those who have done what they could to condemn homosexuality as sinful.

Tax dollars have been used to pay for abortions. Those who have defended the rights of the unborn baby have been stereotyped as a bunch of narrow-minded, bigoted idiots. Indeed, our society has blurred the distinction between good and evil, right and wrong.

There is always the danger that the society around us will determine what we preach rather than God's word. Even preachers can be conformed to the world in the message which they preach, rather than being solely guided by God's word. None of us is above falling into conformity with the world around us. Yet, God's word is quite clear in revealing that what God has spoken is the criterion for determining right and wrong, rather than what society around us is saying. Hence, we need to be especially careful in this moment of time and space to "be not conformed to this world: but be ye transformed by the renewing of your mind" (Rom. 12:2).

Is there yet a clarion voice calling the wicked to repentance? Is there a voice crying in the wilderness, "Repent ye"?

Conclusion

I think that there is yet a host of voices crying in the wilderness of immorality, shouting for men to repent of their wickedness and turn in humble obedience to the Lord. It is true, indeed, that some have muffled their trumpets by compromising in such sinful activities as smoking, social drinking, and mixed bathing. However, I am convinced that the greater number of gospel preachers are still preaching what God's word has revealed on these and a number of other topics.

Brethren, let us hold forth God's word as a light in the midst of this crooked generation. As the lights of denominations become progressively dimmer as they compromise point after point of God's revelation, the world around us will see the pure message of God as we clearly preach it. Those with honest and good hearts will be drawn to this message. Let us not compromise with worldliness but rather reprove it (Eph. 5:11).

NOTES

_____
_____
_____
_____
_____
_____

Questions

True or False

_____ 1. Most of the sins of worldliness are relative.

_____ 2. There are some preachers today who believe that such things as homosexuality and prostitution are not wrong.

_____ 3. There is a tendency for our preaching to be too radical on the subject of worldliness.

_____ 4. The American society has come to accept such things as divorce, social drinking, and dancing.

_____ 5. A preacher should never do anything which might cause people to think he is an "old fogey" for such would harm his influence.

_____ 6. What might be sin for one generation may not be sin for another generation.

_____ 7. A preacher who may not conform to the world in his actions still might conform to the world in his preaching.

_____ 8. Silence is golden when it comes to some areas of worldliness.

Fill In The Blanks

1. Colossians 3:9-10: "_____ not one to another, seeing that ye have put ____ the _____ _____ with his _____; and have put _____ the _____ man, which is _____ in _____ after the _____ of him that _____ him."

2. Romans 1:32: "Who knowing the _____ of _____ , that they which _____ such things are _____ of _____, not only do the _____ , but have _____ in them that _____ them."

3. 1 Corinthians 6:9-10: "Know ye not that the _____ shall _____ inherit the _____ of _____? Be not _____: neither _____, nor _____, nor _____, nor _____, of themselves with _____, nor _____, nor _____, nor _____, nor _____, nor _____, shall inherit the _____ of _____."

4. Ephesians 5:11, "And have no _____ with the _____ works of _____ _____, but rather _____them."

What Would You Do?

1. Suppose you, as a preacher, found out that one of the elder's children had been dancing. You speak to the elder privately about this problem, but the activity continues. What would you do?

   _____

   _____

   _____

2. Several times you have asked the preacher where you attend for a sermon on mixed swimming but he never has preached on that subject. You know that such a lesson is greatly needed. What would you do? _____

_____

_____

_____

3. The elders have announced that they have fired the local preacher. Later, you find out he was fired because of his recent sermon against social drinking. What would you do? _____

_____

_____

_____

CPSIA information can be obtained
at www.ICGtesting.com
Printed in the USA
JSHW050924010323
38333JS00005B/19

9 781584 273981